Your Happy Healthy Pet™

Cavalier King Charles Spaniel

2nd Edition

GET MORE!
Visit www.wiley.com/go/
cavalier_kc_spaniel

Norma Moffat

Howell
Book House™

Copyright © 2006 by Wiley Publishing, Inc., Hoboken, New Jersey. All rights reserved.

Howell Book House
Published by Wiley Publishing, Inc., Hoboken, New Jersey

The publisher and the author make no representations or warranties with respect to the accuracy or completeness of the contents of this work and specifically disclaim all warranties, including without limitation warranties of fitness for a particular purpose. No warranty may be created or extended by sales or promotional materials. The advice and strategies contained herein may not be suitable for every situation. This work is sold with the understanding that the publisher is not engaged in rendering legal, accounting, or other professional services. If professional assistance is required, the services of a competent professional person should be sought. Neither the publisher nor the author shall be liable for damages arising here from. The fact that an organization or Website is referred to in this work as a citation and/or a potential source of further information does not mean that the author or the publisher endorses the information the organization or Website may provide or recommendations it may make. Further, readers should be aware that Internet Websites listed in this work may have changed or disappeared between when this work was written and when it is read.

For general information on our other products and services or to obtain technical support please contact our Customer Care Department within the U.S. at (800) 762-2974, outside the U.S. at (317) 572-3993 or fax (317) 572-4002.

Wiley also publishes its books in a variety of electronic formats. Some content that appears in print may not be available in electronic books. For more information about Wiley products, please visit our web site at www.wiley.com.

Library of Congress Cataloging-in-Publication Data:
Moffat, Norma, date.
Cavalier king charles spaniel / Norma Moffat. — 2nd ed.
p. cm. — (Your happy healthy pet)
ISBN-13: 978-0-471-74823-6 (cloth: alk. paper)
ISBN-10: 0-471-74823-4 (cloth: alk. paper)
1. Cavalier King Charles spaniel. I. Title. II. Series.
SF429.C36M64 2006
636.752'4—dc22
                            2005031900

Printed in the United States of America

10 9 8 7 6 5 4 3

2nd Edition

Book design by Melissa Auciello-Brogan
Cover design by Michael J. Freeland
Illustrations in chapter 9 by Shelley Norris and Karl Brandt
Book production by Wiley Publishing, Inc. Composition Services

About the Author

Norma Moffat bought her first Cavalier King Charles Spaniel as a pet in 1981 and fell in love with the sweet nature and glamorous look of the breed. Since then she has bred and shown more than sixty champions, some of them top-winning show dogs, under her kennel prefix of Brinklow, which is the name of her home village in England. Despite her success with Cavaliers in the ring, she emphasizes that all her dogs are beloved pets first and show dogs second.

Norma has written columns and articles on Cavaliers for the magazine *Dogs in Canada*. She is a life member of the Canadian Kennel Club and past president of the Cavalier King Charles Spaniel Club of Canada. She lives at Brinklow Hill, a ten-acre nature preserve in the woods on the beautiful Niagara Escarpment in Ontario, where the dogs have plenty of room to run and play.

About Howell Book House

Since 1961, Howell Book House has been America's premier publisher of pet books. We're dedicated to companion animals and the people who love them, and our books reflect that commitment. Our stable of authors—training experts, veterinarians, breeders, and other authorities—is second to none. And we've won more Maxwell Awards from the Dog Writers Association of America than any other publisher.

As we head toward the half-century mark, we're more committed than ever to providing new and innovative books, along with the classics our readers have grown to love. This year, we're launching several exciting new initiatives, including redesigning the Howell Book House logo and revamping our biggest pet series, Your Happy Healthy Pet™, with bold new covers and updated content. From bringing home a new puppy to competing in advanced equestrian events, Howell has the titles that keep animal lovers coming back again and again.

Contents

Shopping List

You'll need to do a bit of stocking up before you bring your new dog or puppy home. Below is a basic list of some must-have supplies. For more detailed information on the selection of each item below, consult chapter 5. For specific guidance on what grooming tools you'll need, review chapter 7.

- ☐ Food dish
- ☐ Water dish
- ☐ Dog food
- ☐ Leash
- ☐ Collar
- ☐ Crate

- ☐ Nail clippers
- ☐ Grooming tools
- ☐ Chew toys
- ☐ Toys
- ☐ ID tag

There are likely to be a few other items that you're dying to pick up before bringing your dog home. Use the following blanks to note any additional items you'll be shopping for.

- ☐ _____
- ☐ _____
- ☐ _____
- ☐ _____
- ☐ _____
- ☐ _____
- ☐ _____
- ☐ _____
- ☐ _____
- ☐ _____
- ☐ _____
- ☐ _____

Pet Sitter's Guide

We can be reached at (___)_____-_____ Cell phone (___)_____-_____

We will return on _____ (date) at _____ (approximate time)

Dog's Name _____

Breed, Age, and Sex _____

Important Names and Numbers

Vet's Name _____ Phone (___)___-_____

Address _____

Emergency Vet's Name _____ Phone (___)___-_____

Address _____

Poison Control _____ (or call vet first)

Other individual to contact in case of emergency _____

_____

Care Instructions

In the following three blanks let the sitter know what to feed, how much, and when; when the dog should go out; when to give treats; and when to exercise the dog.

Morning _____

_____

Afternoon _____

_____

Evening _____

_____

Medications needed (dosage and schedule) _____

_____

Any special medical conditions _____

_____

Grooming instructions _____

_____

My dog's favorite playtime activities, quirks, and other tips _____

_____

_____

Part I

The World of the Cavalier King Charles Spaniel

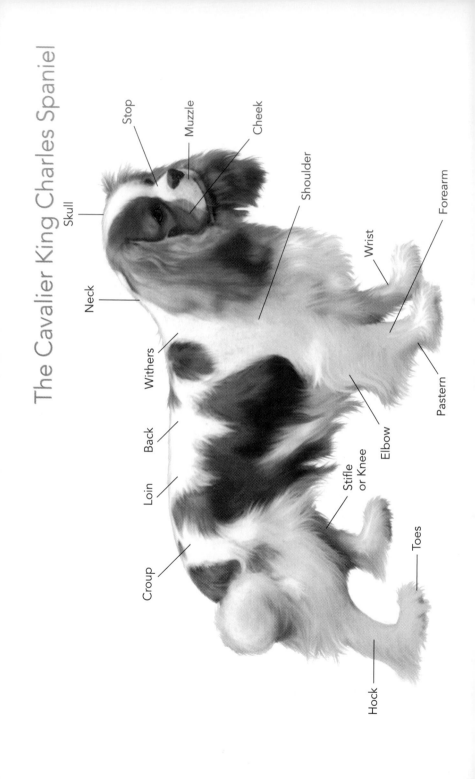

The Cavalier King Charles Spaniel

Stop

Muzzle

Cheek

Skull

Shoulder

Neck

Forearm

Wrist

Withers

Back

Loin

Croup

Pastern

Elbow

Stifle or Knee

Toes

Hock

Chapter 1

What Is a Cavalier King Charles Spaniel?

The Cavalier King Charles Spaniel is a sporting toy spaniel with a sweet, affectionate nature that makes him ideal as a family pet. Happy to be with you no matter what your activity, the Cavalier will love to snuggle on your lap while you watch television but will be equally enthusiastic about keeping you company on a hiking trail. He has all the lively sporting instincts of his larger cousins, but contains them all in a small, portable package.

This little spaniel is immensely adaptable to a variety of lifestyles. He will be at home in the city or the country, and he has but one requirement for his happiness: the companionship and love of a human family. There are so many variations of the human family, and the Cavalier will adapt easily to every one. He is the ideal companion for a retired older person or a couple whose lifestyle includes a daily "keep fit" walk. An active family with children will find the Cavalier affectionate with everyone and always ready for a run or a game of fetch.

Patience with children is a great asset of this breed. I have received a number of photos and e-mails from families that show children and their pet Cavaliers dressed in various costumes. The most amusing was a pretty dog named Cosy in a baby nightdress and frilly cap, complete with a pacifier in her mouth.

It may seem surprising that the Cavalier is also a popular choice for a young working urban couple with a busy life. I always check to make sure they are able to employ a dog walker so that the Cavalier receives enough attention throughout the day. But with this caveat, it can be a great match. These young people tell me that there is nothing like coming home to a Cavalier's loving and enthusiastic welcome after their stressful days at work.

The Breed Standard

Every breed must have a breed standard, which is a blueprint that describes the perfect dog. Most people recognize a specific dog or breed by the dog's appearance. Although personality, temperament, intelligence, and character are vitally important, too, the dog's physical appearance provides people with that important first impression.

The AKC breed standard gives a mental picture of perfect Cavalier conformation, and it is this picture that all serious breeders will endeavor to bring to life in their stock. In this section I'll describe briefly the ideal Cavalier King Charles Spaniel. To read the official breed standard, go to the web site of the American Kennel Club, www.akc.org.

General Appearance

The Cavalier King Charles Spaniel is an active, graceful, well-balanced toy spaniel, elegant and royal in his appearance, with the fearless character of a sporting dog and the gentle, affectionate nature of a true companion. The standard emphasizes that the dog must have no exaggerated features in size or shape and should have a totally natural coat.

The Cavalier King Charles Spaniel should appear elegant and royal, with the fearless character of a sporting dog and the loving nature of a companion.

The lovely, flowing stride of a dog with the correct structure (described in the standard as "free moving and elegant in action") emphasizes the Cavalier's relationship to the larger sporting spaniels and his use as a hunting dog.

When it comes to temperament, the standard says the Cavalier should be friendly, with no tendency to be nervous or shy. Aggressive, bad-tempered dogs are not to be tolerated.

The Body

When fully grown, a Cavalier will stand ten to twelve inches at the highest point of the shoulder (called the withers) and weigh between twelve and eighteen pounds. The body should be just slightly longer

What Is a Breed Standard?

A breed standard is a detailed description of the perfect dog of that breed. Breeders use the standard as a guide in their breeding programs, and judges use it to evaluate the dogs in conformation shows. The standard is written by the national breed club, using guidelines established by the registry that recognizes the breed (such as the AKC or UKC).

The first section of the breed standard gives a brief overview of the breed's history. Then it describes the dog's general appearance and size as an adult. Next is a detailed description of the head and neck, then the back and body, and the front and rear legs. The standard then describes the ideal coat and how the dog should be presented in the show ring. It also lists all acceptable colors, patterns, and markings. Then there's a section on how the dog moves, called *gait*. Finally, there's a general description of the dog's temperament.

Each section also lists characteristics that are considered to be faults or disqualifications in the conformation ring. Superficial faults in appearance are often what distinguish a pet-quality dog from a show or competition-quality dog. However, some faults affect the way a dog moves or his overall health. And faults in temperament are serious business.

than it is tall—more like a square than a rectangle. The chest should be moderately deep, extending down between the elbows to allow plenty of room for the heart. The body should taper slightly behind the ribs, but should not have a tucked-up appearance like that of the Greyhound.

The tail should be carried level with or slightly above the line of the back and should be wagging happily when the dog is moving. Docking the tail— cutting off the end to give the dog a more balanced look—is optional. In Britain, where the practice originated, docking is now illegal. Docking began as a practical measure because the long, fanlike tail of the Cavalier could become tangled or caught in a bush or long weeds when the dog was hunting. Since we in North America own Cavaliers strictly as pets or show dogs, docking is now completely unnecessary. If the breeder does dock tails, no more than one third should be removed and a white tip must be left on the tail of the Blenheim and Tricolor.

The Head

The beautiful head, with its essentially sweet expression and soulful eyes, best expresses the character of the breed. The neck is long, well-muscled, and gently arched at the crest. The head should be in good proportion to the body, with large, round, dark brown eyes that are not prominent and are set well apart. Cushioning under the eyes contributes to the dog's soft and gentle expression.

Cavaliers have long ears with lots of feathering—the silky hair that adds substance and glamour to the ears. The skull is slightly rounded but without a dome or peak, and it should appear flat because of the high placement of the ears. The ears themselves should be set well enough apart that, when the dog is alert, they fan forward to frame the face. The stop, which is the spot on the skull where the muzzle meets the face, should be moderate, and the muzzle itself cushiony, well-tapered, and about one and a half inches long.

The Coat

The coat should be moderately long, silky, and free from curls. No trimming is permitted for the show ring, and the standard says dogs who have been trimmed should be penalized severely. There should be long feathering on the ears, chest, legs, and tail.

This is the only spaniel breed in which the feathering on the feet, known as "bedroom slippers," is left long and untrimmed. Hair growing between the pads and on the bottom of the feet, however, must be clipped away for the comfort of the dog. The emphasis, once again, is on the natural appearance of the dog.

Cavalier Colors

You have a choice of four coat varieties in Cavaliers. Two are known as particolors because they have white markings, and two are known as wholecolors because they have no white markings at all.

Blenheim and Tricolor are the two particolors. The Blenheim has rich chestnut markings on a pearly white ground. The chestnut color must appear around the eyes and on the ears. Between the eyes there is a white mark or blaze. The Tricolor is a handsome black and white dog with body markings placed similarly to the Blenheim, but with bright tan points over each eye, down the side of the cheeks, on the underside of the ears, and under the tail.

The wholecolors are relatively rare, but some breeders prefer them to the particolors, claiming that dogs with these colors are more lively and intelligent. The

Black and Tan Cavalier is, as her name implies, black with the same tan points as the Tricolor. She shares this type of marking with other breeds, including the Doberman Pinscher and Rottweiler, but there the similarity ends. To see a silky, shiny Black and Tan running in a green field is to have a moment of true esthetic enjoyment. The Ruby color of Cavalier is, like that of the Irish Setter, a rich true red all over. As in the world of humans, many owners of Rubies say these red-heads are more volatile but also more fun to live with than the other colors of Cavaliers. In truth, I believe there is not much difference in the temperaments of the four colors. They are all pleasing to the eye, and their sweet nature is such that color is just the icing on the cake.

Applying the Standard

While the breed standard describes the ideal dog, if you are thinking of getting a Cavalier as a pet your two main concerns should be temperament and good health. Although not every Cavalier is right for the show ring, every Cavalier is attractive and the small imperfections that cause a breeder to sell a puppy as a pet rather than a show prospect will not make your dog any less wonderful as a companion. In fact, you many not even see those minor flaws.

Imperfections in temperament, however, are another matter. In this case, settle for nothing less than the sweet dog the standard describes. The temperament of the Cavalier should be as loving and charming as his appearance. For hundreds of years this breed's function has been as a loving companion to humans; this is the greatest gift the Cavalier has to bestow.

From left to right, the colors here are Blenheim, Black and Tan, Ruby, and Tricolor.

Chapter 2

The Cavalier's Ancestry

There has been much speculation about the origin of the Cavalier King Charles Spaniel as we know her today. It is possible that the Cavalier developed from a red and white dog indigenous to Malta or Italy who was crossed with a spaniel-type dog from the Far East in the thirteenth century. Another popular theory is that all spaniels, as their name implies, originated in Spain.

What we do know for sure is that the toy spaniel was refined as a breed in England, and there is no doubt that sporting spaniels were included in the bloodlines of these dogs. From the beginning, the Cavalier has had a dual purpose as both a pet and a sporting companion in the field.

Whatever her origin, it is plain that the Cavalier is a descendant of the "Spaniel Gentle" dogs seen in so many pictures of English lords and ladies from the sixteenth century onward.

The Dog of Royalty

The first recorded royal person who had a beloved toy spaniel was Mary Queen of Scots, and we know this because of a written record of her death. This ill-fated member of the Stuart family was beheaded on the order of Queen Elizabeth I in 1587. It was reported that a little spaniel walked with her, close under her voluminous skirts, to the scaffold and emerged after Mary was dealt her deathblow. The dog would not leave her body until someone picked him up and took him away. He died two days later and was said to have pined away from grief.

Mary was not the only royal to have a toy spaniel. In the Victoria and Albert Museum in London, there is a portrait of King Charles I as a young child. In the fashion of the day (the early 1600s), he is wearing a long dress and is sitting contentedly with a tiny Tricolor Cavalier on his lap.

Charles's love for this breed continued through his lifetime, and Cavaliers appear in many pictures of the royal family from this era. There are two charming paintings by Anthony van Dyck of the children of King Charles I from about 1630. In one, a Blenheim is standing on the right side of the picture and in the other there are two dogs front and center, keeping the children company.

Charles also met the executioner's ax in 1649, as a consequence of the English civil war. It is said that Charles walked to the place of his execution with his black and white toy spaniel named Rogue at his side.

Many of the spaniels depicted from this period look finer in bone (that is, more delicately made) than the Cavaliers of today, and have longer, rather pointed noses. But the fact that they are included in so many paintings of royalty and nobility tells us that the toy spaniel has been kept as a beloved pet and valued for her beauty and personality for hundreds of years.

The Cavalier King

Although kings, queens, lords, and ladies all treasured their toy spaniels, it was after the demise of the Republic and in the restored reign of Charles II in 1660 that the breed became famous throughout the land. Charles was known as the Cavalier King

King Charles II with the little spaniels he treasured. A quote from Samuel Pepys surrounds this illustration.

Staffordshire Dogs

It was due to Queen Victoria's interest in toy spaniels that pottery dogs, known as Staffordshires because of the location of the pottery factories in England, became the rage with the British public. These pottery dogs were made from the late 1850s until the 1930s. The potteries would distribute the white pottery dogs among the cottagers living nearby, and the families—mothers, fathers, and children—would take on the task of painting them. The statues were then collected and the colors fired in. These Staffordshire dogs are not painted realistically at all, but are often done up in bright, fanciful colors courtesy of the local cottagers.

Staffordshire dogs were always made in facing pairs to represent a male and female, and they are easily recognizable as Cavaliers. Throughout Britain, the homes of the working class soon displayed Staffordshire dogs, which were usually placed one at each side of the fireplace. Because they are quite fragile, only a fraction of them survive to the present day.

and his first parliament was dubbed the Cavalier Parliament. He also kept a large number of the little spaniels, who were allowed to follow him wherever he went.

This king was so fond of his pack of little dogs that, according to the famous diarist Samuel Pepys, he neglected the business of the kingdom to play with them. A member of the court, complaining about the general doggy disorder in the royal apartments, declared that the king "took delight in having a number of little spaniels follow him and lie in his bedchamber, where he suffered the bitches to puppy, which rendered it very offensive and indeed the whole court nasty and stinking."

Charles II died a natural death in his own bed in 1685 and was succeeded by his brother James II, who also succumbed to the charm of the toy spaniel. James had occasion to take a sea voyage, and his dogs accompanied him on the ship. A very bad storm blew up and it seemed they were on the point sinking and were preparing to abandon ship. James was heard to cry, "Save the dogs and the Duke of Monmouth!" It seems, in this case, that the toy spaniels had as much importance in the king's mind as his own son, the duke.

Signs of Things to Come

The long-nosed toy spaniel of Charles II's day went out of fashion during the reign of King William III and Queen Mary II, who brought from their native Holland a number of dogs of their favorite breed, the Pug (William III reigned from 1689 to 1702). Perhaps there was some interbreeding between spaniels and Pugs; in any case, a toy spaniel emerged with a domed head and a flat muzzle. This short-muzzled dog was named the King Charles Spaniel and became the type on display at early British dog shows. In North America today, this breed is known as the English Toy Spaniel. Breeders of these dogs would occasionally find a long-muzzled puppy in a litter, but because they considered such dogs unsuitable for breeding, they were sold as pets.

In the early eighteenth century, John, the Duke of Marlborough, had a pack of red and white toy spaniels that he used for hunting pigeon and quail. They were hardy little dogs and the duke recorded that they were well able to keep up with a trotting horse. His estate in Britain was named Blenheim Castle in honor of a great victory he won in 1704 in a war against the French that was fought in the Bavarian town of Blenheim. That is why the red and white variety of the Cavalier became known as Blenheim.

While the duke was away fighting, the duchess was waiting anxiously for news of the battle. She had on her lap a little pregnant spaniel on whose head

The Cavalier's sporting dog origins are evident in their love of water and their good retrieving instincts.

the duchess pressed her thumb while stroking her. When the puppies were born, all bore a chestnut-color imprint of the duchess's thumb, and legend declares this to be the origin of the lozenge or thumbprint mark to be found only on the head of the perfectly marked Blenheim.

Queen Victoria's Cavalier

In the Victorian era (the second half of the nineteenth century), toy spaniels once more came into the public eye because of Queen Victoria's beloved Tricolor spaniel, Dash. He is recognizable in the portraits painted of him as being very like the longer-nosed modern Cavalier. On the very day in 1837 that Victoria was crowned, she recorded in her diary that she came home from this momentous event, changed her clothes, and gave Dash a bath.

When Dash died, the queen herself wrote the epitaph for his tombstone: "Here lies Dash, the favorite spaniel of Her Majesty Queen Victoria, by whose command this memorial was erected. He died on the 20th December 1840 in his ninth year. His attachment was without selfishness, his playfulness without malice, his fidelity without deceit. Reader, if you would live beloved and die regretted, profit by the example of Dash."

Small spaniels with long muzzles had almost disappeared in Britain by the early 1900s. The Cavalier was an attempt by an American to revive the original type.

The Better to Smell You With

Despite the popularity of Dash, the flat-nosed King Charles variety was still the most common in Britain. The reappearance of the original type of toy spaniel, with a face that resembles that of her sporting spaniel relations, must be credited to an American, Roswell Eldridge of Long Island, New York. He went to Britain in the early 1920s to purchase one of the "old nosey type" of spaniel. He felt the English Toy Spaniels were too small and too exaggerated in the shape of the head to be compared favorably to the ones he had seen in historical paintings. He was unable to find the dog he was looking for, however, and was appalled that only the flat-faced spaniels were seen at dog shows.

Eldridge's solution was to offer cash prizes at the famous Cruft's dog show in London, from 1926 to 1931, for what he called "Blenheim Spaniels of the Old Type, as shown in the pictures of Charles II's time, long face, no stop, flat skull not inclined to be domed, with spot in centre of skull." The prize money was 25 British pounds, about $100—a considerable sum in those days. Consequently, there was a renewed interest in producing the old type of toy spaniel among a small group of dedicated English breeders, led by Amice Pitt. When the time came to name this breed to distinguish it from the flat-faced King Charles Spaniel, it seemed logical to call the dog by the name of the Cavalier King, Charles II, who first brought it to prominence. The Cavalier King Charles Spaniel Club was formed in 1928 to promote the re-establishment of the breed.

Cavaliers Re-emerge

There were not many Cavaliers of the "old nosey type" left in Britain, and this situation resulted in a fair amount of close linebreeding and inbreeding by people who were interested in restoring the original toy spaniel as a breed. There are also stories from this era (although no one seems to be able to prove or disprove them) that the Papillon and the Shetland Sheepdog were crossed judiciously with toy spaniels in some breeding programs to bring back the natural muzzle. If, in fact, these stories are true, all we can say is that these breeders were successful in their efforts.

Hard times were coming for the Cavalier and for all purebred dogs in Britain with the start of World War II in 1939. There was food

> Diane Sawyer and her husband, playwright and producer Mike Nichols own and love a Cavalier King Charles Spaniel. I am happy to say that their Tricolor female is one of my own breeding. Brinklow La Bamba Lila is her registered name, and Lila has made a number of appearances on *Good Morning America*.

What Is the AKC?

The American Kennel Club (AKC) is the oldest and largest pure-bred dog registry in the United States. Its main function is to record the pedigrees of dogs of the breeds it recognizes. While AKC registration papers are a guarantee that a dog is pure-bred, they are absolutely not a guarantee of the quality of the dog—as the AKC itself will tell you.

The AKC makes the rules for all the canine sporting events it sanctions and approves judges for those events. It is also involved in various public education programs and legislative efforts regarding dog ownership. More recently, the AKC has helped establish a foundation to study canine health issues and a program to register microchip numbers for companion animal owners. The AKC has no individual members—its members are national and local breed clubs and clubs dedicated to various competitive sports.

rationing, and hardly enough food to keep the human population healthy. Many kennels stopped their breeding programs entirely until the war was over, and the numbers of toy spaniels declined quite drastically. After the war, Pitt and her small group of breeder friends began once more to try to establish lines of the longer nosed toy spaniels that we know today as Cavaliers.

The dog who was to be most influential in re-establishing the ancient breed was Ann's Son, owned by Mostyn Walker, and the original British breed standard was based on his conformation. A written description of Ann's Son by Mrs. Massingham, a well-known breeder and judge, shows great respect for this dog: "A toy spaniel of thirteen pounds, short in the back, entirely flat head, streaming ears to his legs, large dark eyes wide apart, nose long, tipped with jet to match his dark eyes, a white blaze running right up the forehead, thick soft silky coat marked with red and silver Blenheim, and sound as a bell. He was supreme. I realize that it is not only all the perfect points that gave him glory, it was the overall quality which this exquisite little dog had and which shone out of his face that made him Best Ever Born."

What's in a Name?

Until 1945 all toy spaniels, whether flat or long-faced, were officially known as King Charles Spaniels. But once there were a number of the long-faced types in the championship ring, their breeders applied to register them separately. Three women, Pitt, Katie Eldred, and Harper Trois-Fontaines, studied the Kennel Club registrations to determine which dogs should become part of a separate registry for the long-nosed variety. They compiled a list of dogs from which all Cavaliers today are descended. Separate registration from the flat-nosed variety was granted in 1945.

The Cavalier Comes to America

The American history of the Cavalier begins with W. Lyons Brown of the Sutherland estate in Prospect, Kentucky, who brought a dog home from Britain in 1956. With the help of Elizabeth Spalding of Maine, one of the early importers of Cavaliers, and a group of breed enthusiasts, she founded the Cavalier King Charles Spaniel Club USA, which maintains its own stud book (a record of all litters bred) and holds conformation shows for Cavaliers only. This club flourishes to the present day.

In 1994, the American Cavalier King Charles Spaniel Club (ACKCSC) was founded by a group of experienced breeders who wanted to apply for American Kennel Club recognition and registration for Cavaliers. The Cavalier King Charles Spaniel was recognized by the AKC in 1997, and the ACKCSC became the AKC parent club of the breed. A breed standard was submitted and approved at that time. Today, Cavaliers may be seen in show rings throughout the country.

The Cavalier King Charles Spaniel is still a favorite among the British Royalty. This is my own Best in Show Ch. Brinklow Lord Owain the Bard.

Chapter 3

Why Choose a Cavalier?

There are so many reasons why a Cavalier King Charles Spaniel makes a perfect pet and so few that make him unsuitable. First of all, the general appearance of the Cavalier is simply enchanting. He has large, dark, round eyes whose soft expression is a mirror of the soul. His face is plushy, and his beautiful silky coat is a pleasure to touch. When mature, he will have long, feathery ears and a plumelike tail that add the finishing touches to his pretty looks.

The size of the Cavalier is another big advantage, since most people in the United States live in urban areas and either cannot have a large dog or have limited access to open areas or parks for the extensive exercise a large breed requires. Another advantage is that Cavaliers are generally good travelers and are not prone to carsickness.

The Cavalier may also be the best compromise when making the decision of what breed to purchase. In many cases a husband wants a big sporting dog such as a Labrador or a Golden Retriever and the wife wants a smaller dog. A Cavalier King Charles Spaniel is the closest you can come in a small breed to one of the large sporting retrievers. When I tell prospective buyers this, a skeptical look from the husband tells me that he can't believe that this small, silky, stuffed-toy-looking Cavalier is anything like the robust retrievers he favors. It is rewarding for me to discover, after they purchase their Cavalier, that the husband has become absolutely besotted with the dog and now believes every word I said about the Cavalier's sporting nature.

But if I could give only one reason to own a Cavalier, I would emphasize the good temperament of the breed. This little dog is a companion *par excellence*, eager to please and adaptable to any lifestyle. From morning until night, as long as you are home your Cavalier will be gazing at you with those big, soft eyes and will follow you all day no matter what your activity.

Your Dog Needs You

Owning a Cavalier is like having a small, happy child who needs your attention. The Cavalier is so pliable by nature that he will tolerate being left for a few hours while everyone is away from home, but he suffers if separated from his family for too long. A Cavalier is not for you, however, if you and your family are out of your home all day. It is virtually impossible to housetrain a small puppy in this situation. Apart from that problem, the puppy becomes like an abandoned child with no social interaction and none of the gentle discipline that is so necessary to raising a well-adjusted pet. He needs human company more than most breeds and will become depressed if left alone for long periods of time, either inside or outside the house.

Still, if you want to go out for just a few hours, your Cavalier will be content with his own company. Your welcome when you return home will be enthusiastic, to say the least. Remember, though, that now you owe your pet an active hour outside, walking or playing, to keep him happy.

Cavaliers are good travelers and will go where you go.

Gentle Discipline

It is easy to spoil such a sweet and lovable dog, but a Cavalier needs discipline just like any other breed or he will become demanding and will not be pleasant to live with. Having said that, I must emphasize that the very soft nature of this breed means only incentive and reward training should be used. Any physical punishment can ruin the temperament of the Cavalier and make him shy. There is nothing more upsetting to see than a Cavalier who creeps away when company comes, when he should be moving forward with an ever-wagging tail to greet a visitor.

Exercise and Your Cavalier

The exercise requirements of a Cavalier are not excessive, and the breed adapts well to changing circumstances. He requires exercise, as do all dogs, but will enjoy a wide range of activity, from just a good daily walk around the block or in the park to an all-day hike. Although the Cavalier is classified among the toy breeds, he is far from that when it comes to his sporting nature. If you are an outdoor person, the Cavalier is sturdy enough to keep you company in all weather and still be happy at the campsite at the end of the day.

Most Cavaliers, however, will be living in an urban or suburban area where such exercise is not possible. A daily walk is essential to keep your dog in good physical and mental health. Apart from that, several quick outings a day for necessary pees and poops is all that is required.

If you like to start the day with a run or a brisk walk, your Cavalier will keep pace with you. To give your Cavalier the exercise he needs and keep him in good condition, you should walk so that he must trot to keep up with you. If you live in an urban area and your walks are around city blocks, be warned that your Cavalier must be kept on a leash for his own safety, even if you have taken him to obedience classes and he generally stays near you. Any dog can be easily distracted and run across a road to chase a squirrel or greet another dog, even if there are two lines of traffic zooming down the road.

Cavaliers are good retrievers and also love the water.

In a city park, he needs to be on a long line or a retractable leash so you have control. Being a sociable sort, he may want to greet every dog he sees, not realizing that some breeds can be aggressive or protective of their owners. Since he is much smaller than most of the dogs you will encounter, it is simple to reel him in at any sign of danger.

For the person who is limited in physical activity, the Cavalier will adapt to a more sedentary life, and be perfectly happy as long as he is with the person he loves. The Cavalier is also a very good ball or Frisbee retriever, and it takes little effort to stand or sit in one place while your dog does all the running—which provides enjoyment for both of you. In such a situation you may have another member of the family to give him the regular exercise he needs, or you may decide to hire a professional dog walker.

> **A Burglar's Friend**
>
> There is no guard instinct in the Cavalier. Although he will bark when someone comes to the door, it is a bark of excitement rather than warning. He will greet any visitor with enthusiasm, and I believe that he will welcome a burglar as long as that burglar makes a fuss over him.

Hunting Instincts

If you are in a fenced area where your dog can be taken safely off the leash, you will notice that although he runs free, he will keep an eye on you to be sure you are within reach. Given a large, grassy, open area, the Cavalier will naturally quarter the field, running diagonally back and forth with his nose low to the ground. His hunting instincts are in full play as he picks up the hundreds of scents wafting upward.

The Cavalier also confirms his sporting origin by being a very good retriever if encouraged early. Of our ten dogs, five are natural retrievers, bringing back a ball or catching a Frisbee with great enthusiasm. My 3-year-old Blenheim girl, Joy, is amazingly skillful not only in her ability to retrieve on the fly and bring a ball to hand, but also to find one that other dogs have lost in deep grass or bush. If a dog has lost a ball, and I have some idea of its vicinity, I point to the area and give Joy the command "find it." She will search that patch of ground over and over until I tell her to stop. Very often she finds the ball in a short time and comes trotting over proudly, tail held high and eyes sparkling, to present it and be told how very clever she is.

This Cavalier King Charles Spaniel displays the classic stance of a hunting dog.

A Water Dog

If you spend time where there is access to water, you will soon discover that your Cavalier, like other spaniels, is a real water dog. The first sight of an expanse of water causes great excitement. Your Cavalier will tiptoe in and stand there for a

Those hairy ears must be cleaned often and kept dry to avoid infections.

while. Then a genetic light in his brain seems to switch on and away he goes, swimming as though he has done it all his life.

I brought Daphne, my 5-month-old Tricolor puppy, up to our summer home on a lake for the first time one July. She didn't know what to make of the water at first and stood on the shore barking, telling me how foolish I was to be paddling in the shallows. Then I teased her with a ball and threw it just a few inches into the water. She pounced with glee, causing a great splashing. Then I threw the ball a little further. In no time, Daphne was swimming and retrieving like a veteran. After a few days, Daphne would run down to the water by herself early in the morning while the lake was misty and placid and take a long, leisurely swim just for the fun of it.

One word of caution about the ears is necessary here. Adult Cavalier ears are very hairy, even on the inside. It is essential to keep them dry to avoid infections. The easiest way to deal with this is to dry the ears with a towel to get rid of the excess moisture, lift each ear, and use a hair dryer on a "cool and low" setting to dry the inside gently and thoroughly. If your dog is in the water regularly, you must accustom him to the hair dryer early and often so that he does not take fright at the noise and the rush of air.

The All-Weather Cavalier

I am often asked if the Cavalier needs a jacket or sweater to keep warm through cold winters. It is true that because dogs live in centrally heated houses, they do not grow thick coats for the winter. In general, though, the Cavalier does not need to be dressed to go out in even the coldest weather, as long as he is being active. Leaving him out in the yard by himself on a very cold day is a sure way to give him a chill, but as long as he is walking with you or generally is on the move, his activity will keep him warm enough.

In southern climates, you may need to have your Cavalier clipped to keep him comfortable on hot days. Once a Cavalier has been spayed or neutered, there will be accelerated coat growth. The texture will change from relatively short and silky to long, thick, and rather woolly, and the dog will need to be taken to a groomer regularly.

Some Charming Habits

If you are not exercising regularly and vigorously with your dog, it is important to limit his diet so that he does not become overweight. Remember that a fat Cavalier is an unhealthy one and, as with humans, fat and lethargic dogs are prone to the early onset of progressive heart disease.

You must resist the urge to give your Cavalier treats from the table. It is so hard to ignore those begging eyes, but the Cavalier is prone to put on weight easily, and this applies particularly to females. A few small, good quality dog biscuits first thing in the morning are all that is needed to keep your dog going until his daily meal, which should be fed in the late afternoon or early evening.

Dinnertime is a highlight of the Cavalier day and a time when he will get excited and tend to bark and jump up on you and anyone else in the vicinity. Teach him when he is very young to sit and wait for his food or for any treat.

The Cavalier Stretch

Perhaps you like to sit and read the morning paper after breakfast. Your Cavalier will come to you and perform what I call the Cavalier Stretch. He will put his two front feet on your thigh and stretch his whole body and head upward as a sign of affection. This is a definite breed trait, which even young puppies will display. You can pet him a little or give way completely and invite him onto your lap.

In the old days, when people traveled by horse and carriage, a lady would take a cozy little spaniel on her lap to help keep herself warm during a winter trip. Thus, the nickname of the toy spaniel in those days was the "Spaniel Gentle" or "Comforter," a dog considered pretty enough and civilized enough to be a constant companion for any lord or lady.

Snoring and Snorting

The occasional Cavalier turns out to be a snorer. The culprits seem to be those individuals who have shorter than average noses. We have a Ruby girl named Dina, now 9 years old, who has a deep, reverberating snore worthy of a Labrador Retriever. At first the noise was bothersome, but now we are so used to it that we consider it a lullaby. In any case, we don't think the snoring is a serious enough problem to deny her bed privileges.

There is another minor behavior associated with the structure of soft palate and uvula, called snorting, and this usually happens when the dog is excited. To the uninitiated, it seems as if the dog is struggling for air as he makes loud, snorting noises with his mouth shut. There is no danger to the dog, though, and the behavior will subside on its own with no ill effects. If your Cavalier is a snorter, you can help him to stop by closing off his nostrils with your fingers so that he has to open his mouth to breathe. As soon as he opens his mouth, the snorting will stop.

Scooting

You have a house full of company and want them to meet your little canine treasure. In comes your elegant, aristocratic Cavalier and begins to scoot his bottom along your best oriental carpet, rear legs held high in the air—a rather disgusting demonstration. No, he does not have worms or impacted anal glands; this is a breed trait that starts in puppyhood, and one we have learned to live with. All you can do is distract the dog to stop his performance, and this is

Cavaliers are so "terminally cute" that we forgive their funny habits.

easily done by a quiet word. He will soon remember his manners and work his charm on a roomful of people, going from one to the other to give a greeting and get a pat in return.

Your Bed Is My Bed

At the end of the day, the Cavalier is totally convinced that your bed is where he belongs. When a puppy leaves my house, I tell the new owners to start as they mean to go on, and if they want their dog to sleep in his own crate or bed, that must be done starting on the very first night, and every night after. Nine times out of ten I will get a phone call in which the new owner will say something like this: "We took the crate into our bedroom and put him in it, but he whined and cried, and his eyes looked so sad that we couldn't stand it. As soon as we put him up on the foot of the bed he settled right down and we didn't hear a peep out of him all night."

A Cavalier makes an excellent bed dog and fits his silky body perfectly into the bend of your knee. The only problem is that he may occasionally have a desire to express an excess of affection in the middle of the night. He will creep up the bed and press himself against your mouth and nose, cutting off your air supply. Your dreams may be suddenly filled with a sensation of suffocation and you'll wake with a start to find little precious showing you how much he loves you. This is a small price to pay for a companion whose uncritical affection, merry disposition, and charming ways make your life so much happier.

The Dog's Senses

The dog's eyes are designed so that he can see well in relative darkness, has excellent peripheral vision, and is very good at tracking moving objects—all skills that are important to a carnivore. Dogs also have good depth perception. Those advantages come at a price, though: Dogs are nearsighted and are slow to change the focus of their vision. It's a myth that dogs are colorblind. However, while they can see some (but not all) colors, their eyes were designed to most clearly perceive subtle shades of gray—an advantage when they are hunting in low light.

Dogs have about six times fewer taste buds on their tongue than humans do. They can taste sweet, sour, bitter, and salty tastes, but with so few taste buds it's likely that their sense of taste is not very refined.

A dog's ears can swivel independently, like radar dishes, to pick up sounds and pinpoint their location. Dogs can locate a sound in $6/100$ of a second and hear sound four times farther away than we can (which is why there is no reason to yell at your dog). They can also hear sounds at far higher pitches than we can.

In their first few days of life, puppies primarily use their sense of touch to navigate their world. Whiskers on the face, above the eyes, and below the jaws are sensitive enough to detect changes in airflow. Dogs also have touch-sensitive nerve endings all over their bodies, including on their paws.

Smell may be a dog's most remarkable sense. Dogs have about 220 million scent receptors in their nose, compared to about 5 million in humans, and a large part of the canine brain is devoted to interpreting scent. Not only can dogs smell scents that are very faint, but they can also accurately distinguish between those scents. In other words, when you smell a pot of spaghetti sauce cooking, your dog probably smells tomatoes and onions and garlic and oregano and whatever else is in the pot.

The Cavalier and Children

One of the questions I am frequently asked is whether this breed is a good one to have when there are children in the family. The answer is a qualified yes, depending upon the children. The average Cavalier is so affectionate and forgiving of the slightly rough treatment that can be handed out by children, but his patience is not endless.

A puppy usually goes to his new home at the age of 8 weeks, when he weighs between three and five pounds. If there are toddlers or small children in the family, they must be supervised when playing with the puppy, and they must never be allowed to pick the puppy up and walk around with him. I have seen a few disasters as a puppy wriggles and jumps out of a child's arms and is injured in the fall. The floor is the perfect place for child and puppy to be together, as it is safer and less intimidating for the puppy to have someone at his own level. When you see that the puppy has had enough play with the child and is beginning to back up or run away, pick him up and put him in his place of refuge, the crate, for a nap or quiet time.

I always ask a family to visit if they are interested in purchasing a puppy, and the reason is that I want to meet the children to assess their behavior with the dogs. Children who pay attention to my instructions on how to approach the dogs and who are gentle with them will usually treat a puppy with respect. Little horrors who grab at the dogs and run around making loud noises with no discipline from their parents will probably end up making a puppy nervous.

The temperaments of some puppies are more suited to children than others. All ranges of temperament in the Cavalier should be sweet and loving, but they vary, just as temperaments do in a human family. The extroverted, confident puppy will be happy with the noise and activity generated by a house full of children, while this situation would be intimidating for the quiet, submissive puppy, who would be better suited to a home with adults only.

Some puppies are better suited to children than others. And some children are better suited to dogs than others.

Chapter 4

Choosing Your Cavalier

You have purchased this book, and that means you already know that careful research and preparation is the only way to be sure you get a family pet who will be a joy in your life. Your new dog will be a vital part of your life for the next decade or more. It's important, then, to make sure you choose your Cavalier wisely. There are many places to find a Cavalier King Charles Spaniel, and some are definitely better than others.

Reputable Breeders

Finding a reputable breeder of Cavaliers takes careful research, and your efforts in this regard will be well worthwhile. The definition of a good breeder is one who, first of all, takes excellent physical and social care of the dogs they own. Next in importance is the emphasis the breeder places on the good health and temperament of the dogs they produce. A reputable breeder will be taking young dogs they are thinking of breeding to AKC conformation shows to prove that these Cavaliers are close to the breed standard and are able to obtain AKC championships. AKC judges are indeed well qualified to determine if a dog is worthy of championship points, but in the end it is the breeder who has the picture of the perfect Cavalier in their mind's eye, and it is they who are striving to produce that picture in the flesh. A reputable breeder has studied the genetics of the breed, health-tested all their breeding stock and chosen the sire and dam of each litter carefully to complement one another.

Since the Cavalier is such a versatile little dog, some breeders also enter their Cavaliers in other canine activities, such as obedience or agility trials, where owner and dog must work as a team. When a breeder is willing to spend their time in this way, since any training is quite intensive, you know that they really love their dogs and want to see them use their minds as well as their bodies.

You want to get a puppy from someone who will be there for you in the future. A reputable breeder will be readily available to answer questions for you as your puppy grows up. On your visit to the kennel, the breeder will introduce you to the dam (mother) of the litter and

> ### CAUTION
>
> When making appointments, for the breeders' sake please do not visit more than one kennel in the same day because it is an easy way to spread disease. For instance, if there is an outbreak of kennel cough in one place, the infection can be transferred by you on clothes or shoes to the next kennel you visit. Kennel cough is not dangerous to the healthy adult dog, but it can be deadly for baby puppies.

perhaps the sire (father) as well. It may be that the breeder has used a fellow breeder's dog at stud. In this case, the sire will not be on hand, but you should be able to see his pedigree, picture, and a copy of his health clearances. This information will give you a good idea of your future puppy's temperament and eventual size as an adult.

Although it's impossible to predict the future, you will be able to take some comfort that the breeder has done everything possible to make sure you have a strong, healthy, well-adjusted puppy. Your puppy will have been introduced to friendly people and will have heard a variety of household sounds. She will have had her first worming and first set of vaccinations. You will not be allowed to bring her home before 8 weeks of age, and some breeders will want to keep the puppy until she is 12 weeks old and has had her second vaccinations.

Finding a Breeder

How do you find a reputable breeder? The first step is to get in touch with as many breeders as possible in your area and arrange a visit for the whole family. The Cavalier King Charles Spaniel Club USA and the American Cavalier King Charles Spaniel Club both have breeder referral resources (their contact information is in the appendix), as does the American Kennel Club. If you have a friend or neighbor who has a healthy, well-behaved Cavalier, you might want to ask them for the name and telephone number or e-mail address of their dog's breeder. You can also attend dog shows to meet Cavalier breeders. A word of caution is necessary here: Never approach a breeder/exhibitor at a dog show when they are about to go into the ring, but only after the competition when both exhibitor and dog are more relaxed.

Reputable breeders test the quality of the dogs they produce by entering them in canine competitions, such as this agility trial.

First Contact

E-mail is an easy and inexpensive way to get in touch with breeders, but I recommend that you actually telephone to get some impression of the personality and knowledge of the breeder. If you are satisfied with the information you get, the next step is to make an appointment to meet the dogs.

Most reputable breeders do not have puppies available for sale. Litter size in Cavaliers is relatively small—an average of three. Also, reputable breeders do not keep a lot of dogs because Cavaliers should be living in the house with their owners and puppies should be born in the house, either in the kitchen or in a room the breeder has designated for this purpose.

Beware if the breeder tells you they have a large stock of Cavalier puppies to choose from. This information may well be the first sign that this is a large commercial breeder, a puppy mill, or that the so-called breeder is actually selling puppies as a middleman or broker. Puppies from such a source often come from unregistered stock, possibly not purebred, and have been raised in poor conditions with no socialization.

A good breeder will invite you to visit so they can to meet you to determine if you will provide a suitable home for a Cavalier. You will also have the opportunity to decide whether this is the breeder from whom you want to purchase a puppy.

What to Look For

When a kennel visit has been arranged, here are some questions to ask and points to consider:

- The breeder's house and surrounding area should be well kept and clean.
- There should be no doggy smell when you enter the house.
- Ask if it is possible to meet all the dogs. The dogs should be friendly enough to receive visitors happily.
- Do the dogs have the run of the house? If not, can you actually visit the rooms they live in? This will tell you a lot about the environment in which they are raised.
- Are all the dogs happy and sociable?
- Are the dogs well groomed?
- Have the sire and the dam of the litter had health checks for genetic disease?
- Does the breeder have a purchase contract?
- What kind of health guarantee comes with a puppy?
- Are all the dogs registered individually as purebred with the American Kennel Club, The Cavalier King Charles Spaniel Club Inc. USA, or the Canadian Kennel Club? (These are the only three registry bodies that are acceptable in the USA and Canada.)

A reputable breeder will also have questions for you. He screens the people who come to buy his puppies because he's concerned about the pups' future. He may ask you to fill out an application, ask for references, and will certainly want

The area where the puppies are kept should be safe and clean.

to know if you have owned dogs before. If you don't sound like an ideal Cavalier owner, he will not sell you one. His decision is not about you as a person, but about the best home environment and living conditions for his puppies.

Waiting for Your Pup

After visits to several breeders, you may well decide which one you would like to deal with. If there will not be a puppy available in the near future, ask if you can put your name down on a list, and then wait as patiently as you can. If you find that two or three of the breeders you have visited are good people from whom to buy a puppy, you may wish to go on those waiting lists as well. This way, if the litter you are waiting for does not happen, or if there are deaths among the puppies, you will still be in line for a pup. It is best to tell these breeders that you are on more than one list, and when you know definitely that you are going to get a puppy from a specific breeder, let the others know right away.

Puppy, Adolescent, or Adult?

If you can't decide whether you want a puppy, an adolescent, or an adult, know that each age has its pros and cons. It is easier to acquire a young puppy 8 to 12 weeks of age, but there is an intensive housetraining, socialization and behavior training period that will require much of your time for at least the first six months. Puppies begin to shed their baby teeth at the age of four and a half months, and your possessions, particularly leather shoes left on the floor, will be fair game for those sharp chewing needles. As with a young child, all hazards must be removed from a puppy's environment, and you must know where your puppy is and what she is doing all the time.

If you haven't the time or facilities to cope with a very young puppy, an adolescent or a young adult may be more suitable. Cavalier puppies are much in demand, and since pet-quality puppies usually go to their new homes early, obtaining an older one requires a much longer search. Occasionally a breeder will keep a puppy for six to twelve months to see whether she will meet

Young pups benefit a great deal from being with their littermates and their mom, and should not go to their new homes before they are at least 8 weeks old.

Cute as they are, puppies are also a lot of work. Sometimes an adolescent or an adult dog is the right choice.

the requirements of the show ring. If she does not measure up for this purpose, then the breeder will let her go to a pet home. The advantage here is that the older puppy or adolescent is already housetrained, has had regular grooming and socialization, and has generally become a good canine citizen. This essential early training is compensation enough for missing the very cute and cuddly stage of the small puppy's life.

If you decide that an adult Cavalier is your choice, there are advantages and disadvantages. On the plus side, what you see is what you get: The size, the pretty face with its big brown eyes and sweet expression will be the same for life. An adult is housetrained, has had all her vaccinations, and is used to interacting with people and coping with the general commotion of family life. Provided that an adult has lived in a normally run home with plenty of affection, she is easy to live with and will have no destructive habits. If the adult Cavalier is from a reputable breeder, she should have no problems adapting to your home.

You will find a great variation in price when it comes to puppies, adolescents, and adult Cavaliers. Young puppies from 8 weeks and adolescents up to a year or so old are the most expensive. Depending upon the age of the adult, price usually decreases as dogs grow older. It is not uncommon for a reputable breeder to place their retired dogs in pet homes, and in this case, the price is usually minimal because all the breeder wants for the dog he has loved and nurtured is a happy home for the rest of her life.

Why Spay and Neuter?

Breeding dogs is a serious undertaking that should only be part of a well-planned breeding program. Why? Because dogs pass on their physical and behavioral problems to their offspring. Even healthy, well-behaved dogs can pass on problems in their genes.

Is your dog so sweet that you'd like to have a litter of puppies just like her? If you breed her to another dog, the pups will not have the same genetic heritage she has. Breeding her *parents* again will increase the odds of a similar pup, but even then, the puppies in the second litter could inherit different genes. In fact, *there is no way to breed a dog to be just like another dog*.

Meanwhile, thousands and thousands of dogs are killed in animal shelters every year simply because they have no homes. Casual breeding is a big contributor to this problem.

If you don't plan to breed your dog, is it still a good idea to spay her or neuter him? Yes!

Adopting from a Rescue Group

Purebred rescue groups are organized by local breed clubs or simply by groups of people who love their breed. These people want to save homeless dogs from death at local shelters and find them permanent, loving, knowledgeable homes. Rescue groups also participate in educational activities, usually on a local level, teaching people about their breed of choice.

Finding a Cavalier rescue group is easy. The web sites of the Cavalier King Charles Spaniel Club USA and the American Cavalier King Charles Spaniel Club list rescue groups, and you can find many local breed rescue groups online. Most breeders have contact information for rescue groups in their areas, and many shelters can refer you to breed rescue. Each rescue group is independent and the adoption policies vary somewhat from group to group.

The homeless dogs are usually kept in foster homes where they are evaluated for temperament and physical health, are spayed or neutered, vaccinated, and

When you spay your female:

- You avoid her heat cycles, during which she discharges blood and scent.
- It greatly reduces the risk of mammary cancer and eliminates the risk of pyometra (an often fatal infection of the uterus) and uterine cancer.
- It prevents unwanted pregnancies.
- It reduces dominance behaviors and aggression.

When you neuter your male:

- It curbs the desire to roam and to fight with other males.
- It greatly reduces the risk of prostate cancer and eliminates the risk of testicular cancer.
- It helps reduce leg lifting and mounting behavior.
- It reduces dominance behaviors and aggression.

trained. People who wish to adopt a dog go through an application process much like that for a reputable breeder. An application is required, as are references. A home inspection is usually required, as well.

You should ask the volunteer with the rescue group questions, too: Where do the dogs come from? How much do you know about the dogs you foster? How long do the dogs stay with a foster home? Do you know whether the dogs are good with kids, other dogs, or other pets? Are the dogs spayed or neutered? Vaccinated? Microchipped?

Before Cavaliers are ready for adoption they should be checked by a veterinarian, given all vaccines, spayed or neutered, and tested for heartworms and any other medical conditions. A behavior expert in the group should evaluate each rescue dog to make sure she has a stable personality. There is usually a small fee to adopt, but it hardly ever covers the on-going costs of the rescue operation.

If the dog is being placed from a Cavalier rescue organization, they will have done a lot of screening and will be able to give you all the necessary information about the dog's background. It may be that the dog has ended up with a rescue group because there has been a separation in a family, or her owner moved away and was unable to take the dog with him. In these cases, the dog may have some habits that would not suit you, such as sleeping on the bed or begging for treats from the table. It is more time-consuming to correct these habits in an adult, but the old adage, "You can't teach an old dog new tricks" is simply not true. Any bad habit can be altered with patience and consistent training.

Rescue groups are also very good about following up after the adoption. If you need help or simply have questions, the group will be there for you.

Where Not to Get a Cavalier

If you go on the Internet and type in the name of the breed, you will find hundreds of web sites. Be aware that any Cavalier breeder, whether reputable or not, can put up an attractive web site. You will need to screen these breeders, as I have already described. Never buy a puppy sight unseen. Anyone who offers to sell you a dog without ever having met you is not a reputable breeder.

Backyard Breeders

A backyard breeder is someone who produces puppies for sale but does not have the knowledge (or desire, or energy, or finances) to do what is necessary to produce the best dogs possible. This could be someone who has a female Cavalier and simply breeds her to the nearest Cavalier male he can find—perhaps to another pet down the street who has not been neutered, or he may even crossbreed her with a dog who just looks as though he may be a Cavalier. The backyard breeder may not be able to give you any proof of the puppies being purebred or registerable with any kennel club. He has done no health or temperament checks and can tell you nothing about the dogs in the puppies' background.

Backyard breeders may produce some nice puppies. But they are just as likely to produce dogs with problems. In addition, once the puppies are born, the backyard breeder rarely knows what nutrition and exercise the puppies need to grow up well. They may not be handled enough or correctly, may not have the socialization they need, and may not have their first sets of shots. Backyard breeders often sell their puppies as soon as they are weaned, which may be between 5 and 6 weeks of age; it is far too soon for the pups to leave their mother and littermates. The backyard breeder rarely has a waiting list for his puppies, and as they get older, they are often turned over to the local shelter.

Why Not Buy from a Pet Store?

The only advantage to buying a Cavalier from a pet store is that you can have a puppy the day you walk in. There are many disadvantages. A pet store does not sell adults or rehome abandoned dogs. They're selling Cavalier puppies strictly to make a profit, and their source might be puppy mills where these poor babies are produced en masse for the market without regard to any other consideration.

You will also pay a lot more than you would from a breeder. You won't be able to see where or how the dog was raised, you're unable to meet the dog's relatives to see if they are the kinds of dogs you would want to have, and you won't know the dog's health history. Pet store employees won't be able to show you how to groom your dog and cannot answer any questions you have as the years go by. And if you have to rehome the dog, a pet store will never take her back. A reputable breeder will always stand behind your purchase because the Cavalier's welfare is his first concern.

Sex and Color

Are you flexible as to the sex and color of the puppy you want to buy? Nine times out of ten, when I get an inquiry the potential puppy buyer will say, "I want a Blenheim female." It seems there is an old wives' tale that females make better pets than males, but this is definitely untrue concerning the Cavalier. Males in this breed are just as sweet natured and devoted as females, if not more so.

I believe this general bias against males is based upon the notion that they lift their legs to urinate on everything vertical and that their urine is strong-smelling as they mature. A good breeder will require you to neuter your puppy, and this will certainly take care of the sex-related behavior of the male, since, when the hormones are no longer working he will not have the same urge to pursue females or mark his territory.

All puppies are pretty, and the boys and girls are equally sweet.

Part II

Caring for Your Cavalier King Charles Spaniel

Chapter 5

Getting Ready for Your Cavalier

In the excitement of getting your new Cavalier, don't forget that there is much preparation you must do *before* those little paws begin to patter around your kitchen. A visit to a pet supply store, with its vast array of merchandise, is quite bewildering unless you have a firm idea of the basic items you will need.

The box on page 47 lists the essentials you will need to have on hand when your dog comes home. Some of them deserve a closer look.

The Crate

The first essential is a suitable crate, which will provide your puppy with a safe haven and you with an excellent tool for housetraining. Remember that your four-pound puppy will grow to an adult size of about eighteen pounds and will measure about twelve to thirteen inches at the withers (the top of the shoulder). The crate you buy should be sized for the adult, so you will not have to buy a bigger crate as the puppy grows.

There are two types of crates, and both have their advantages. A metal wire crate is a good choice for the kitchen because that is usually where the family spends a lot of time. Your puppy will have company and will be able to see what is going on in all directions, while you will be able to notice if he is getting restless and needs to be whisked outside to do his duty. If you want to keep your puppy in the bedroom at night to reassure him and to monitor his need to go out, the folding type of metal crate is ideal; it folds down quickly and easily to be taken from place to place.

Puppy Essentials

You'll need to go shopping *before* you bring your puppy home. There are many, many adorable and tempting items at pet supply stores, but these are the basics.

- **Food and water dishes.** Look for bowls that are weighted in the bottom so they will be harder to tip over. The diameter of the bowl should be just wide enough to take the adult Cavalier's muzzle comfortably, but not so wide that the ear feathers end up in the bowl every time your dog eats or drinks. Stainless steel bowls are a good choice because they are easy to clean and impossible to break. Plastic is also unbreakable and convenient, but never comes completely clean and is therefore less sanitary. Avoid bowls that place the food and water side by side in one unit—it's too easy for your dog to get his water dirty that way.
- **Leash.** A six-foot leather leash will be easy on your hands and very strong.
- **Collar.** Start with a nylon buckle collar. For a perfect fit, you should be able to insert two fingers between the collar and your pup's neck. Your dog will need larger collars as he grows up.
- **Crate.** Choose a sturdy crate that is easy to clean and large enough for your puppy to stand up, turn around, and lie down in.
- **Nail cutters.** Get a good, sharp pair that are the appropriate size for the nails you will be cutting. Your dog's breeder or veterinarian can give you some guidance here.
- **Grooming tools.** Different kinds of dogs need different kinds of grooming tools. See chapter 7 for advice on what to buy.
- **Chew toys.** Dogs *must* chew, especially puppies. Make sure you get things that won't break or crumble off in little bits, which the dog can choke on. Very hard plastic bones are a good choice. Dogs love rawhide bones, too, but pieces of the rawhide can get caught in your dog's throat, so they should only be allowed when you are there to supervise.
- **Toys.** Watch for sharp edges and unsafe items such as plastic eyes that can be swallowed. Many toys come with squeakers, which dogs can also tear out and swallow. All dogs will eventually destroy their toys; as each toy is torn apart, replace it with a new one.

For travel in the car, a plastic or fiberglass crate is a safer choice. Its solid, smooth surfaces will provide better protection for the puppy in case of a sudden stop or an accident. There is quite a variation in the quality of plastic crates, and I recommend that you get a really heavy-duty one with a metal mesh door—it may be more expensive, but it will not break with constant use.

A Pad for the Crate

There are all sorts of pads made to fit most crates. The most important feature of a pad for a crate is its ability to stand up to constant washing and drying. Some crate cushions have an inner and an outer cover. The inner one cannot be washed and is filled with substances such as cedar to repel fleas. These have a zippered outer cover that can be removed for washing. I recommend the all-in-one, totally washable pad because it is really more hygienic to be able to put the whole thing in the washer and be sure it is clean right through.

A puppy will enjoy having his own nice cozy cushion in any room of the house. One bed I recommend you avoid is the wicker basket with a cushion. The puppy will inevitably chew on the wicker, which will splinter badly. A sharp piece could pierce your puppy's tongue or mouth, or, if ingested, could get stuck in the stomach or intestines.

Confining Your Puppy

Having settled the matter of the puppy's crate and pad, the next consideration is what equipment you need to let him out of the crate but still keep him in a confined area of the house. The kitchen is ideal because of its washable floor, and if there is no door between the kitchen and other rooms of the house, a baby gate will be indispensable to prevent the puppy from bouncing all over the house, to the detriment of your rugs.

Even if there is a door to the kitchen, you can leave it open and install a baby gate because the puppy will be able to see you through the gate and be reassured by your presence. A shut door is an invitation to the puppy to scratch to attract your attention.

A plastic pressure-fitted baby gate with diagonal mesh is probably the best kind for this purpose, since a wooden one is just too tempting for a chewing puppy. Beware of a wooden gate with vertical slats—a

TIP

It is important that a well-filled water dish be wherever your puppy is. There is a special water dish designed for a crate or pen that sits in its own holder and can be adjusted to the puppy's height as he grows.

puppy can get his head stuck between the slats, causing panic and injury. Most baby gates have a spring release, one-handed operation, which makes them easy to open and close. If the mechanism is awkward or difficult to operate, you may find yourself climbing the gate instead, which increases your own likelihood of getting hurt.

An alternative to the baby gate is an enclosed exercise pen that can be set up in the kitchen with the puppy bed at one end and thick newspapers at the other—just in case. Between the bed and the newspapers, place a towel lengthwise so the floor of the exercise pen has good traction for the puppy's feet and so he will not slip on the kitchen floor and strain his young joints and legs.

"Ex" pens are made of six or eight wire mesh foldable panels, some with doors and some without.

Your dog will need safe, comfortable confinement both indoors and out. This is a portable outdoor crate.

A door is preferable, so the puppy does not have to be lifted in and out, but it does add to the cost of the pen. A pen two feet high is about right for the Cavalier and for you. Any higher and those panels can be hard on the midriff when you bend over to pick up your puppy. The ex pen offers the advantage that the puppy is totally confined and unable to get into any hazards while you are out. He can only get to the things you put in the pen.

Other Essentials

Other essential purchases are water and food bowls, and there are many to choose from—plastic, porcelain, or stainless steel. The porcelain ones are usually prettily decorated but very breakable, while the colorful plastic ones are eminently chewable. That leaves the stainless steel bowls, which, although not pleasing to the eye, are not only indestructible but can be put into the dishwasher and made thoroughly sanitary.

What's a Snood?

As your puppy loses his fluffy baby coat and begins to grow those lovely long ears that frame the face, you may want to buy him a snood to wear while he is eating, so that his ears will remain clean. The snood is a kind of little elasticized hat that you pull on over his nose and eyes to the top of the head to hold the ears up and out of the food. They are available at many pet supply stores. They have the added charm of making your Cavalier look like a little Victorian lady in a mob cap. You must begin using the snood very early in the puppy's life so that he gets used to the routine of having it put on before he eats.

When selecting a water or food dish, remember that your Cavalier will grow long, feathered ears. A deep, rather narrow bowl is preferable to a wide one that allows the ears to be covered in whatever the dish holds, whether food or drink. A dish four to five inches wide and about four inches high is ideal.

Collar and Leashes

Pay a little visit to your puppy at the breeder's home about a week before he is due to come home to you. Measure the circumference of his neck with a piece of string, and then you will have no trouble selecting the right size collar. Buy him a flat nylon adjustable collar that has room to expand, with a quick-release plastic buckle. While his coat is relatively short, this type of collar is suitable, but when he begins to grow long hair as an adult, a rolled nylon or leather collar is preferable to avoid cutting the coat. A four- to six-foot leash about the same width of the collar should be perfect because it is the type of leash used in most puppy training classes. Collar and leash sets come in every shade of the rainbow, to say nothing of snazzy embroidered sets. You can have fun deciding which of these will enhance your puppy's looks and personality.

Have an identification tag made for the collar with your name and telephone number on it, in case the puppy strays and gets lost.

You should get a retractable leash, which will give your puppy some freedom of movement while keeping him under control. These leashes have a plastic

A six-foot leather leash is a great training tool.

handgrip and a nylon running line twelve to twenty-six feet long. The line will automatically extend and retract as your puppy runs away from you and back again. If there is a sudden emergency, you can stop the line by applying the thumb-operated brake, and you can then reel him in quickly.

Toys!

A small Kong provides an excellent way for your puppy to pass the time. It is a hard rubber toy with an irregular shape and a hole on the underside. With peanut butter spread inside, or stuffed with some other treat, it will have your puppy licking and chewing with enjoyment for hours. Kongs are also great for throwing and retrieving because they bounce unpredictably, giving your puppy the pleasure of the chase. Best of all, a Kong is totally scrubbable, and you can clean all of the inside with a bottle brush.

A hard rubber ball is perfect for the game of fetch, but be sure the ball is large enough that it can't get stuck in the puppy's throat and small enough for him to get a good grip on it.

One inexpensive toy I have found that is wonderful for puppy play and encourages retrieving is a child's splash ball. These are the size of tennis balls, made for children to soak with water and throw at each other. They are polyester

Safe, interesting toys are not optional—all dogs need them.

filled and covered with nylon material, very light to handle and spongy soft. Because they are so light, when a puppy pounces the ball will skitter off to entice the puppy to pounce again. When he does pick it up, it is so soft he can carry it easily. Ariel, a Blenheim puppy now seven months old, is addicted to the splash ball. She will carry it around all day, as a child will carry a favorite doll, and offer it to any visitor to throw for her.

A toy that costs you nothing and provides a lot of enjoyment is a pair of old wool socks tied together. A puppy will carry this around, growling and shaking it as if it were alive. Another good type of plaything is a tug toy, which is ideal for play between you and your puppy—but don't leave him alone with it. The tug toys are usually made of cotton or nylon, tightly braided, so the puppy cannot ingest any large amount, but it is wise to err on the side of caution and take it away when you have finished your game of tug-of-war.

Toys to Avoid

Toys to avoid are those made of soft plastic or those that have squeakers in them, unless you are there to supervise the play. Many an owner has suffered grief after a teething puppy chewed off a large piece of plastic or a squeaker and swallowed it, thus blocking the intestine. Soft plastic toys made in the shape of steaks, hot dogs, and cute figures are gimmicks made to appeal to dog owners, but the puppy's safety is paramount.

Outdoor Puppy-Proofing

The box on page 54 explains how to protect your home from your puppy and your puppy from your home. After you've worked on that list, it's time to look around your yard to be sure it is also puppy-proof. Whether you have a small yard or a garden, you need to take a walk around the perimeter fence looking for small openings or spaces where an adventurous Cavalier puppy could squeeze through. If there is any space between fence and ground, you can be sure that the puppy will find it. He will squeeze his nose into the smallest gap and then wiggle his way under the opening like a snake.

Do you have a prized flower or vegetable section of your garden? If so, fence it off with some chicken wire. Freshly turned soil is an invitation to digging for your Cavalier, which will mean a trip to the bathtub for him and rescue of your upended plants. Cavaliers are not constant diggers, but the smell of well-cultivated soil is irresistible to most dogs. If your puppy makes holes in your lawn, you can thwart him easily. Fill the hole with his poop and cover it with a thin layer of earth. I guarantee he will not go back to dig in that hole again.

If there are certain plants in your yard you want your puppy to stay away from, you will have to physically fence them off in some way.

Puppy-Proofing Your Home

You can prevent much of the destruction puppies can cause and keep your new dog safe by looking at your home and yard from a dog's point of view. Get down on all fours and look around. Do you see loose electrical wires, cords dangling from the blinds, or chewy shoes on the floor? Your pup will see them too!

In the kitchen:

- Put all knives and other utensils away in drawers.
- Get a trash can with a tight-fitting lid.
- Put all household cleaners in cupboards that close securely; consider using childproof latches on the cabinet doors.

In the bathroom:

- Keep all household cleaners, medicines, vitamins, shampoos, bath products, perfumes, makeup, nail polish remover, and other personal products in cupboards that close securely; consider using childproof latches on the cabinet doors.
- Get a trash can with a tight-fitting lid.
- Don't use toilet bowl cleaners that release chemicals into the bowl every time you flush.
- Keep the toilet bowl lid down.
- Throw away potpourri and any solid air fresheners.

In the bedroom:

- Securely put away all potentially dangerous items, including medicines and medicine containers, vitamins and supplements, perfumes, and makeup.
- Put all your jewelry, barrettes, and hairpins in secure boxes.
- Pick up all socks, shoes, and other chewables.

In the rest of the house:

- Tape up or cover electrical cords; consider childproof covers for unused outlets.
- Knot or tie up any dangling cords from curtains, blinds, and the telephone.

- Securely put away all potentially dangerous items, including medicines and medicine containers, vitamins and supplements, cigarettes, cigars, pipes and pipe tobacco, pens, pencils, felt-tip markers, craft and sewing supplies, and laundry products.
- Put all houseplants out of reach.
- Move breakable items off low tables and shelves.
- Pick up all chewable items, including television and electronics remote controls, cell phones, shoes, socks, slippers and sandals, food, dishes, cups and utensils, toys, books and magazines, and anything else that can be chewed on.

In the garage:
- Store all gardening supplies and pool chemicals out of reach of the dog.
- Store all antifreeze, oil, and other car fluids securely, and clean up any spills by hosing them down for at least ten minutes.
- Put all dangerous substances on high shelves or in cupboards that close securely; consider using childproof latches on the cabinet doors.
- Pick up and put away all tools.
- Sweep the floor for nails and other small, sharp items.

In the yard:
- Put the gardening tools away after each use.
- Make sure the kids put away their toys when they're finished playing.
- Keep the pool covered or otherwise restrict your pup's access to it when you're not there to supervise.
- Secure the cords on backyard lights and other appliances.
- Inspect your fence thoroughly. If there are any gaps or holes in the fence, fix them.
- Make sure you have no toxic plants in the garden.

Make Time for Your Puppy

It is important that someone in the family be able to be at home during the first early weeks when the puppy needs the most attention and instruction. It is a crucial period, because from 8 to 16 weeks of age the puppy is a little learning sponge, soaking up all the information and acquiring the habits that will last a lifetime.

Time spent with a young puppy will pay off in good behavior and good citizenship for life. There is nothing sadder than a new puppy being left at home alone while everyone is out of the house during the day. Apart from the fact that he is desperately lonely and pining for company, when someone does come home, he will go mad with excitement and be difficult to control.

An entire family at work or school all day has only a couple of hours in the morning and a few at night, and little time to give a puppy the socializing and training he needs. Families with children, in particular, have busy evenings and weekends with group activities of all kinds. Look carefully at your schedule to see if you really have enough time to devote to your dog. If you can't be there yourself, can you hire a dog walker or a neighborhood teenager who loves dogs

Cavaliers are not the kind of dogs who can be left alone all day in the yard. They need a lot of time with you.

and needs a part-time job? As a breeder, I have a firm policy never to sell a Cavalier to anyone if there is nobody home during the day.

The Big Day

Now that the matter of providing time for the puppy has been dealt with, you are just waiting for the day when you can make your Cavalier a member of the family. When that day arrives, pick up your puppy in the morning so that he has the entire day to get used to his new people and location. A puppy brought home in the evening and put to bed in an unfamiliar house all by himself is liable to make a fuss about the abrupt change. He has never been alone in his life; his mother and his littermates have always been there to snuggle up with and make him feel secure.

Puppies in general, and Cavaliers in particular, benefit from a regular schedule during the day, which helps immensely with housetraining. On arriving home with your puppy, carry him from the car to the spot in the backyard where you want him to do his business. It is likely that he will want to relieve himself, and when he does, praise him immediately.

Puppies are natural followers because they are pack animals. Encourage him to follow you into the house and to the kitchen where you have set up his living area. Playing on the floor at puppy level is the best way to begin the social interaction that makes the special link between a Cavalier and his family.

Impress upon everyone who is going to play with the puppy the importance of not getting him overexcited. Supervise children whenever they play with him to be sure that neither they nor the puppy has a bad experience.

Puppy Chewing

Think of your puppy as a little person with no hands but plenty of small, sharp teeth. He will learn about your world through chewing anything and everything, and will not discriminate between his chew toys, furniture and carpets, your shoes, and your favorite CD—indeed, anything chewable left within reach. And that includes human fingers.

As soon as your pup closes his jaws on you, leave your hand or finger in his mouth but give a loud high-pitched scream. The noise will startle him and he will let go. The very instant he lets go, praise him. Next, offer your finger or hand to him to see if he will try again. If he does, go through the same routine. The key is not to pull your hand away, and this is sometimes difficult to teach to children, but it is well worth persisting with this method of bite-proofing the puppy.

The prime time for chewing on objects is when he begins to cut his second permanent teeth at the age of about 4 months. If you see him put his teeth on

Your Cavalier is eager to please and will need your gentle guidance to learn what you expect from him.

something not his own, say "ach!" to draw his attention and then distract him with one of his own chew toys. If he is attracted constantly to one item of furniture or one set of shoes, you can smear a tiny amount of hot pepper powder on it and he will certainly avoid that item in the future. Pet supply stores also carry commercial sprays for this purpose.

Do not use physical discipline with Cavaliers. They are soft by nature and can be easily cowed or frightened by such action. In some cases, a puppy so disciplined can become nervous and shy of you and possibly all people.

The exception to this rule is when there is a direct danger to young puppies, such as a potential shock from a plugged-in electrical cord within reach. A shock from one of these can kill a small Cavalier puppy, and it doesn't take more than a few bites to get through the insulation. If it is an emergency situation and you must act, then shout and swoop the pup up in your arms to remove him from the hazard. Right away after that, distract the puppy's mind from the fright this may cause by giving him a tasty treat. I find that the tip of your finger coated thickly with peanut butter is just the ticket.

Naptime

When the puppy seems tired from his introduction to house, new family, and playtime, put him into his crate for a nap. Never let anyone wake him up to play with him. He needs to sleep his tiredness away as human babies do, and if woken frequently at the whim of children, will become nervous and cranky. When he wakes up, he will want to go to the toilet and will probably cry to get out of the crate because it is a puppy's nature to try to keep his bed clean.

When your dog cries to get out, carry him again to the chosen spot outside. Cavalier puppies are toy size and their bladders and intestines are correspondingly small. While your puppy is awake and playing, he will have to relieve himself every twenty minutes or so. Getting him out frequently is the key. (See chapter 10 for more on housetraining your dog.)

A sleeping puppy can go through the night for six hours or so without having to be taken out. The pattern of crate time and play, interspersed with three meals a day at this age, is a routine your puppy will adapt to quickly, and he will become so attuned to it that he will soon be able to tell you that you are late with his dinner by dancing around and asking for it.

When you put your new puppy to bed on his first night in your home, you will set a pattern for the rest of his life. It is not fair to exile him to a crate in the laundry room or basement where he is totally alone, feels abandoned, and cries his little heart out. The best routine is to take his crate into your own bedroom so that you can reassure him that he is not alone and to be aware if he needs to go out in the night.

On the other hand, you may have decided that this puppy is to have the privilege of sleeping at the foot of your own bed with the idea that if it was good enough for King Charles II, it's good enough for you. In our house the dogs take turns on our bed, two at a time. The rule is that both must sleep on the same side and must not creep up above our elbows. In fact, Cavaliers do love to work their way up the bed to your face, and many would love to sleep curled around your head if you would allow it, rather like little Cavalier bonnets. Whatever your decision, the idea is to have the puppy somewhere near you at night because he needs to know you are there and ready to care for him.

Visiting the Veterinarian

After a few days of settling into his new routine, take your Cavalier puppy to see your veterinarian for a general check-up. There should be no problems, but if veterinarian does turn up anything, the breeder should be the first person to know about it. In such a case it is a good idea to ask the breeder to talk directly to your veterinarian. While you are investigating veterinarians, always ask about their after-hours emergency services.

Chapter 6

Feeding Your Cavalier

Apart from a good set of genes and a strong constitution, what determines the health and longevity of your Cavalier is nutrition. Over the years, I have discovered that more problems develop from oversupplementation rather than lack of nutrition. We are so concerned about getting everything right, giving a puppy all she can eat, adding oil supplements to give her a shiny coat, or taking the word of a friend that this or that will give a dog optimum health. As with everything in life, we must find a balance.

Dry Food vs. Natural Food

Large commercial dog food companies spend millions of dollars and do the feeding trials necessary to be sure their food is nutritious and will be suitable for the average dog. Still, if you were to offer the average Cavalier a bowl of dry dog food and a bowl of chopped meat, which do you think he would choose?

Adding Meat and Veggies

Meat by itself is not sufficient. In the wild dogs eat the partly digested vegetable contents of an animal's stomach, and that, along with the rest of the carcass (including the skin and bones), provides a complete, natural diet. Our dogs are totally dependent upon what we provide for them, so how do we give them as close to a natural diet as possible? As with all else, compromise is the key.

In addition to a top-quality dry kibble food, I always add a couple of tablespoons of ground or chunk meat and one teaspoon of raw pureed vegetables, all mixed together with a little water. Any leftover veggies will do—except onions, which contain toxins. A dog cannot digest the cellulose in raw whole vegetables, but if you puree them, her digestive system can make good use of them and the natural vitamins and antioxidants they contain.

About once a week I feed organ meats such as liver or chicken giblets and hearts to provide a more natural balance of meat and to get closer to the food a dog would find in the wild.

Cooked Meat or Raw?

There is some controversy as to whether the meat should be raw or cooked. I prefer to feed raw meat because it is the canine's natural food and is digested more completely than cooked meat. In hot climates, however, and for safety, many people prefer to cook the meat. In thirty years of feeding dogs, I have never had a problem with raw meat, but I am extremely careful to make sure it is fresh and that any uneaten portion is thrown out right away.

If you wish to feed raw ground or stewing beef or boneless chicken or fish, it is best to buy a pound at a time, then divide it into small portions that can be frozen and pulled out of the freezer on the day of use. If you are a pet owner and have just one Cavalier, the cost of fresh meat at the supermarket is a small outlay to be sure your dog is getting good-quality food.

A healthy, balanced diet will keep your dog fit and active throughout her life.

Ingredients Good Enough to Eat

When selecting a dry food for your Cavalier, read the ingredients list on the label. For a puppy or an active adult, meat should be the first ingredient because it provides essential protein. Protein levels vary from 15 percent for older dogs to 26 or 28 percent for puppies. On the whole, 21 to 23 percent protein in dry food is suitable for the adult Cavalier. It is not advisable to give a high-protein food to any adult dog unless the dog is working hard for her living. A protein count well over 23 percent will cause an adult Cavalier's excretory organs to work overtime getting rid of the excess protein and put too much stress on them. I tend to avoid dog foods with a grain base of corn or wheat, since some Cavaliers can be sensitive to these and produce loose stools in consequence. Whole grain ground brown rice, barley, or oats are all good grain components and are well tolerated by Cavaliers.

I never use canned dog food because it has a wet, gummy consistency and sticks to the dog's teeth, which can be a prime cause of tooth decay. Also, since the meat is not considered fit for human consumption, who knows how good it is? The protein count of canned dog food is rarely in excess of 10 percent, which is not high enough to provide good nutrition in itself. Add to that the artificial flavors and sometimes revolting smell of canned dog food, and I recommend that you avoid it and buy meat for your Cavalier that is fit for human consumption.

A puppy needs three meals a day, with enough food for her to gain weight steadily as she grows.

Dog food labels are not always easy to read, but if you know what to look for they can tell you a lot about what your dog is eating.

- The label should have a statement saying the dog food meets or exceeds the American Association of Feed Control Officials (AAFCO) nutritional guidelines. If the dog food doesn't meet AAFCO guidelines, it can't be considered complete and balanced, and can cause nutritional deficiencies.
- The guaranteed analysis lists the minimum percentages of crude protein and crude fat and the maximum percentages of crude fiber and water. AAFCO requires a minimum of 18 percent crude protein for adult dogs and 22 percent crude protein for puppies on a dry matter basis (that means with the water removed; canned foods should have more protein because they have more water). Dog food must also have a minimum of 5 percent crude fat for adults and 8 percent crude fat for puppies.
- The ingredients list the most common item in the food first, and so on until you get to the least common item, which is listed last.
- Look for a dog food that lists an animal protein source first, such as chicken or poultry meal, beef or beef byproducts, and that has other protein sources listed among the top five ingredients. That's because a food that lists chicken, wheat, wheat gluten, corn, and wheat fiber as the first five ingredients has more chicken than wheat, but may not have more chicken than all the grain products put together.
- Other ingredients may include a carbohydrate source, fat, vitamins and minerals, preservatives, fiber, and sometimes other additives purported to be healthy.
- Some grocery store brands may add artificial colors, sugar, and fillers—all of which should be avoided.

Feeding a Growing Puppy

How much food is right for your Cavalier? A young puppy needs three meals a day, and she should be allowed to eat all she can in about ten to fifteen minutes. After that, pick up the dish and keep any remaining food in the refrigerator until the next meal, or dispose of it and start afresh. The exception is a puppy

Milk

Adult Cavaliers do not actually need milk in any form, except the pregnant female who can benefit from the extra calcium. Cow's milk should not be fed to dogs because the type of lactose it contains is not digestible and will probably cause diarrhea. Goat's milk, however, is readily digestible by both young and old, and I have never seen a case of stomach upset when using it. Goat's milk in the quart size is becoming commonly available in supermarkets, and it is carried in many health food stores.

who adores her food and soon becomes very fat. She should not be given the opportunity to eat as much as she likes but should get measured meals until she slims down a little, and then should be given enough to maintain a slow and steady weight gain. Too much weight put on too quickly will certainly put undue strain on a puppy's growing frame.

On the opposite end of the scale is the young puppy who is a poor eater. This is rare in Cavaliers, but it can happen. In this case, do not worry that she is starving herself. Hand feeding or tempting your little darling with luscious treats such as boneless chicken breast is an absolute no-no. If you do this, you will create a situation in which your puppy will soon demand to be hand fed all the time with food fit for a queen. Be tough and steel yourself not to give in, even if you think she is getting too thin. Make up the puppy's dish as instructed, put it down, and if she does not eat, pick it up in about fifteen minutes. Puppies will not starve themselves. The primary instinct to eat and survive will always win out, and eventually your fussy baby will begin to eat normally.

You will notice, at about the age of 4 months, that your puppy will begin to pick at one of those three meals, instead of eating with enthusiasm. When this happens, you know it is time to put her on two meals a day—one in the morning and one in the evening. The same general rule applies about letting her eat all she can in a limited time.

Once she is past 6 months of age, you can safely put her on an adult meal of about one cup of food a day in the late afternoon or early evening, with just a snack of a biscuit or two in the morning. Whether you feed your dog once or twice a day is your decision, but if you do feed twice a day, be sure that you only give half the day's ration at a time or you will soon have a blimp on your hands.

Keeping an Adult in Good Weight

Now you must use the "rule of eye and hand," which means you should be able to see your Cavalier's waist just behind the ribs and you should be able to feel the ribs, but not see them. A good general rule for an adult Cavalier is to feed one to one and a half cups of food a day, depending upon the kind of physical exercise she gets. If your Cavalier begins to look like a sausage with no shape to her body, cut down on the food right away. A fat Cavalier is one whose life will be short and unhealthy, because of the genetic tendency in the breed to heart disease (see chapter 8).

Females, in particular, are very good eaters and use their food efficiently, and so are prone to put on weight easily. I have several Cavalier girls who thrive and look just right on two-thirds of a cup of food a day.

You may find that giving your dog two tiny meals a day, each totaling half the usual quantity, is easier on both you and the dog. A good "filler" for fat but hungry Cavaliers is a raw carrot, which they will demolish with enthusiasm but which will be expelled at the other end exactly as it went in.

It is unusual for a Cavalier to be a picky eater, but it does happen occasionally and it is usually a male who has this problem. My advice for the adult dog is the same as that for the fussy puppy: Stick to one good brand of dry dog food, mixed with a small amount of meat and vegetables as described before, put the dish down, and pick it up after fifteen minutes whether it is empty or not.

Make sure you count all the training treats you feed your dog when you are figuring out her daily ration.

The adult dog may go for more than twenty-four hours without eating more than a bite or two, but don't give in. Throw out what has not been eaten and give her another meal at the proper time. Above all, don't tempt her with any special goodies and don't give her any treats whatsoever, because then she will expect these all the time and will turn her nose up at the regular fare.

Keep the Oldies Slim

Most Cavaliers past their middle years will be less active, and this is a good reason to take special care not to overfeed your dog. The food should also contain little or no salt.

When I was a novice breeder and more experienced people told me that spayed or neutered dogs put on weight more easily, I thought that was just an old wives' tale. Now I know that what they said is true. It seems that when the hormones are not present, the metabolic processes change and any weight

Seniors do have a tendency to put on weight, so take care not to overfeed.

gained is hard to lose, particularly if the dog is past middle age. This does not mean you should not spay or neuter your pet-quality dog (the many advantages of spay and neuter are outlined in chapter 4), but it does mean you should watch her weight carefully.

A good-quality food designed for seniors is all that is needed for the older dog who is still in good health. If she is not as interested in her food as she formerly was, give her two small meals a day with a little extra meat to spark her appetite.

If your veterinarian diagnoses a heart or kidney condition, or if your dog is getting fat on the food you are using, the vet can prescribe a special diet designed for these problems. I supplement my older dogs with antioxidant vitamins E and C, along with their regular ration of dry food, raw meat, and pureed raw vegetables. Continue to give your dog treats that are hard and chewy to stimulate the teeth and gums.

Even though the dog is eating normally, you may notice that she is losing weight or drinking more often than before. Excessive thirst may be a sign of diabetes, and any weight loss without a ready explanation should be checked out by a visit to the veterinarian.

What About Bones?

You will find that although your Cavalier enjoys her food, she will still have the need to chew. Modern forms of dry dog food do not allow for the kind of chewing that is beneficial to teeth and gums. But the question of whether to give bones to Cavaliers is very controversial. Some breeders swear by bones and some breeders swear at them.

After thirty years in dogs and nearly twenty-five in Cavaliers, the only type of bone I will allow my Cavaliers to have is a piece of raw beef shank marrow bone. There is no danger of splintering with this bone, and the dogs have the added satisfaction of being able to lick the nutritious marrow out of the middle. I

> **TIP**
>
> If you are traveling in the car, there is an ingenious plastic water dish commonly known as a "water hole." It has a small opening in the top just big enough for your Cavalier's muzzle to go in easily, and a wide rim with a curve down toward the center. The "water hole" type of dish can be carried uncovered in the car, and it won't spill over when the car is in motion.

have the butcher cut the shank into pieces one to two inches long. I keep them in the freezer and take them out on the day I wish to feed them. My dogs have them as a treat once a week, and it keeps them happy for at least an hour's good gnawing.

The great advantage is that while bones satisfy a dog's desire to chew, they also clean the teeth and tone up the gums, preventing the onset of gingivitis. From a sanitary point of view, beef marrowbones must always be taken away and thrown out once the dog has licked the marrow out of the middle and had a good chew. No other bones of any description should be given to a Cavalier because of the danger of splintering and internal injury.

Never give your dog cooked bones. They can be deadly; they will splinter into sharp shards if chewed and can easily pierce the stomach or intestines.

Other Chewing Options

Cavaliers absolutely adore the pig's ear chewy treats that are available at every pet supply store, and I must confess to buying these occasionally. The problem is that they are very greasy and will make a mess of Cavalier ears, unless you have trained your dog to tolerate a snood.

Hard dog cookies will provide some jaw exercise, but since the Cavalier is prone to put on weight, these must be strictly limited. Dog cookie manufacturers add extra flavorings and sugar to make their products tasty, but the calories in one cookie can be really detrimental to an already pudgy Cavalier.

Rawhide provides some good chewing, but I urge you to buy a really large single rolled piece, not one that is made up of little pieces twisted together, which can be separated and swallowed in chunks. The danger here, of course, is that a piece ingested whole will cause an impaction in the gut. Some people really object to the slimy mess that the end of a rawhide roll becomes when well chewed. Yes, it is rather repulsive, but rawhide to the dog is like chocolate truffles to the human.

Dangerous Treats

On the subject of dog treats, there are so many kinds marketed to appeal to the owner rather than the dog, including some that are advertised as "chocolate drops." This treat is not chocolate but a carob substitute that can be well tolerated by dogs. In fact, real chocolate must never be used as a treat because it contains the chemical theobromine, which can be toxic to dogs.

One Christmas my daughter's Cavalier, Trixie (inclined to be fat and known to be a clever food thief), discovered a one-pound box of very expensive chocolates and scoffed the lot. The family was out at the time, and they came home to find poor Trixie feeling quite sick and sorry for herself, but alive. The reason she survived was that she had promptly vomited her stolen meal all over the living room Persian carpet.

Another food to beware of is cheese. In very small slivers, it can make a good little treat. But large pieces, such as cheddar or mozzarella, can be dangerous and get caught in your dog's throat and choke her.

Water Is Essential

We cannot leave the subject of feeding your Cavalier without mentioning the importance of readily available water to help your dog's digestive processes. I cannot emphasize enough the essential nature of water for the dog. Your dog can survive for days without food, but not without water.

Wherever your Cavalier is, whether in your kitchen, in your car, or visiting friends, always have fresh, clean water sitting in a bowl nearby so that she can slake her thirst. When you are visiting, always take water from home for your pet. As with humans, a change of water can sometimes cause stomach upsets or diarrhea, and this can be avoided by always carrying a bottle of water with you.

Dogs must have access to fresh water at all times. This girl has her own travel bowl.

Chapter 7

Grooming Your Cavalier

The Cavalier is a natural breed and requires minimal—but regular—grooming to keep him looking his best. The coat of an unneutered animal is medium in length, with long feathering on the ears, chest, legs, tail, and feet. The coat is straight, silky, and easy to care for, and is often referred to as "wash and wear" by breeders.

The AKC breed standard does not allow any trimming of show dogs. Neutered or spayed pets, however, will have a much longer coat that is finer and thicker, rather more like cotton than silk. This coat requires more work to maintain, and some trimming may be needed.

The Right Equipment

Before we discuss the actual process of grooming, let's talk about the tools you will need to do the grooming easily and efficiently.

Combs

The best type of comb for a Cavalier is a small metal one, about five inches long, half set with wide-spaced teeth and the other half set with more closely placed teeth. This type of comb may be advertised in pet supply catalogs as a *cat* comb. The wide tooth half is good for general combing, and the end with more closely set teeth can be used for combing out the fine hair behind the ears and to pull out fleas if you ever have a summer infestation.

When you go to the store to buy a comb, run your fingers over the ends of the teeth. They should not feel sharp to the touch, but should be rounded so that they do not tear the coat.

Brushes

You'll need three brushes, each with a different function, to groom your Cavalier. The first is a pin brush. This brush is about seven inches long from end to end, and has an oval head with a rubber cushion inset with metal pins. If you only buy one brush for your Cavalier, the pin brush is the one to have because it is used most often in general grooming.

Next comes the slicker brush, which has a rectangular head covered with very fine bent pins, like a carding comb. Cavalier ears and feathering tangle easily, and the slicker brush will encourage all those tangled hairs to lie in the same direction, which makes combing them much easier.

Last comes the finishing touch, a bristle brush. The other brushes prepare the coat so that it lies flat and tangle free, but the bristle brush is the one that will provide that silky sheen so pleasing and typical of the Cavalier coat.

Nail Clippers

There are two types of nail clippers: a guillotine type with one blade where you put the nail through a small opening and then squeeze the handles to chop it off; and a clipper type with two cutting edges. I find the clipper type much easier to use. Unless you have a very steady hand, it is easy to put too much of the nail through the hole in the guillotine type and cut into the *quick*—the bundle of nerves and blood vessels that runs through the center of the nail. It is very difficult to use this tool with a dog who objects to the process. The two-blade clipper works like a scissors and some have a guard so that you cannot cut the nail into the quick.

Scissors

The Cavalier is a natural breed and should be left untrimmed, but it is allowable to cut off excess hair on the bottom of the foot, even on a show dog. Long hair left to accumulate between the pads will mat and form a slippery cushion, giving the dog poor traction. It will also retain water, which is unhealthy for the pads since they should dry off quickly to avoid bacterial infections between the toes. The exception to the no-trimming rule is the neutered or spayed animal whose coat is long and very thick. In this case, a pair of thinning shears is useful to make the coat easier to groom and more comfortable for the dog.

Small scissors with rounded ends are the best solution for trimming under the feet. If you cannot find them in a pet supply store, you may very well come across them in your supermarket's baby supply section, where they're sold as baby nail scissors.

Grooming Table

A grooming table is a sturdy little metal table covered with rubber matting that provides a washable surface and gives the dog secure footing. It comes with a grooming arm—metal tubing that extends up from the table and then across it. From the grooming arm hangs an adjustable dog collar, which holds the dog in place while allowing you to keep both hands free for grooming. It's a good idea to get a grooming arm that has a C-clamp to fix it to the table.

Although a table of this kind is not essential, it does make the job of grooming so much easier. The grooming arm holds your dog in place, and the table raises him up off the ground so you do not have to bend over.

A word of caution is necessary here: Never leave your dog alone even for a minute while he is in the collar of the grooming arm. If he attempts to jump off the table, he could easily injure or even strangle himself.

> **Grooming Tools**
>
> Metal comb with wide teeth and fine teeth
>
> Pin brush
>
> Slicker brush
>
> Bristle brush
>
> Nail clippers
>
> Scissors with rounded ends
>
> Thinning shears
>
> Grooming table
>
> Grooming spray
>
> Canine shampoo and conditioner
>
> Tear stain solution
>
> Ear cleaning solution
>
> Canine toothbrush and toothpaste

Grooming Spray

Since you should never groom a Cavalier coat when it is dry, because this will break the hair, a grooming spray is essential to dampen the coat. There are many to choose from in pet supply stores, but the one I prefer is a skin conditioner as well as a grooming spray. It contains tea tree oil (*Melaleuca alternifolia*), which is healing for the skin and has the added benefit of discouraging fleas and mites, which are repelled by the scent. There are also sprays specially made for sensitive skin that contain aloe vera or other soothing ingredients. It is well to experiment with several types of grooming spray to determine which one is best for your dog.

Don't forget the ear cleaning solution when you go shopping for grooming supplies.

Shampoo and Conditioner

It is important that you do not use shampoos and conditioners made for humans on your Cavalier. The pH level of the dog's skin is different from yours, and what is suitable for you may be highly irritating for him. Whatever canine shampoo you select, be sure it is gentle and not drying to the coat. My favorite has a base of coconut oil, which gives a lovely sheen and a pleasant lingering scent.

The main purpose of conditioners is to keep down static, tame the flyaway coat, and help to prevent tangles. I have often simply used the grooming spray liberally after the bath in lieu of conditioner, since it does basically the same job.

Toothpaste and Toothbrush

Cleaning the teeth is an absolutely essential part of the grooming process for a Cavalier. The muzzle is relatively short, yet contains the same number of teeth as that of a German Shepherd or any other large breed, and the teeth are packed closely together. Cavaliers are also prone to gingivitis. If unhealthy bacteria accumulate around the teeth and gums, they will migrate to the valves of the heart and can cause serious damage there.

Doggy toothpaste and toothbrush come in a kit, which can be purchased at the pet supply store. Toothpaste comes in several different flavors that appeal to dogs, such as brewer's yeast, liver, and beef. Never use toothpaste made for

Regular tooth brushing is an important part of every dog's grooming regime. You can use a special canine toothbrush, a rubber finger stall, or even a piece of clean gauze wrapped around your finger.

humans on a dog. The taste would be repellent to them, and after all, they cannot rinse and spit.

The toothbrush has a big brush at one end and a small one at the other to accommodate any size canine mouth. The pet supply store will also carry a rubber fingerstall for the same purpose, for those dogs who object to having a brush in their mouth. The fingerstall has little rubber bumps on it that will providing a massaging action for the teeth and gums.

I cannot overemphasize the importance of cleaning the teeth regularly.

Grooming a Puppy

Although your Cavalier puppy will need very little grooming, if any, go through the process regularly—every day if possible—from head to tail. This way, he will become accustomed to the routine and then, when he is grown, you will have no trouble at grooming or bath time.

If you have no objection to using the kitchen as a location, the kitchen sink and counter are an ideal height for grooming your puppy. Otherwise, the laundry tub and counter will do, but the laundry tub usually requires that you bend over for some time while washing and rinsing, and it can be hard on your back. Use a rubber mat on the counter or in the sink so the puppy does not feel nervous about standing on a slippery surface. The type of rubber mat you can buy to put in a bathtub is perfect for this. The puppy may not be happy being so far off the ground, but you can reassure him with a gentle but firm grip and soothing words. He may struggle and try to jump off the table, so be sure to keep one hand on his collar while you groom him with the other.

You want to make the grooming process a pleasant experience for the puppy. Begin by spritzing his body lightly with the grooming spray. Start combing at his head, then gently down the ears and progressing down the body. Repeat this process with the bristle brush. Lift the ear flaps to make sure the insides of the ears are pink and glistening and that there is no sign of debris or redness. Lift each of his feet in turn, just so he gets used to having them handled, which will make it easier at nail-cutting time.

Now go back to the head and see if there is any stain or debris at the inner corners of the eyes. Cavalier eyes are so large and round that the tear ducts sometimes cannot take all the flow of tears that is necessary to keep the eye clear, and they overflow. If there is staining, wipe the area with a cotton ball dampened with saline solution, but if there is dried debris you may need to use the fine-tooth comb to get it out, then the damp cotton ball. If tearing stains are problem, there are commercial products available that will clear them up.

Holding the puppy's mouth lightly shut, insert your finger gently inside the cheek and rub it along his gums and teeth on both sides. When he gets used to this, you can put a little dog toothpaste on your finger and then eventually you will be able to insert a brush or fingerstall to clean his teeth.

Remove just the tip of the nail when you clip. This is guillotine-style clipper.

Cutting toenails can be stressful for a puppy, but it must be done regularly—about once every two or three weeks. If you do not keep the toenails short and they grow long and curl over, the whole balance of the leg will be thrown off. Taking off just a tiny amount of nail often is far less stressful than leaving them to grow for a month and struggling with the puppy because he is not used to the process. You will know when the puppy needs to have his nails cut because you will be able to hear them click on a wood or tile floor.

Now that grooming is over, the time comes to decide whether the puppy needs a bath. I am not a believer in bathing when it is not absolutely necessary. If the puppy looks dirty or smells dirty, then go ahead; otherwise regular, thorough grooming is enough to clean the coat and spread the natural oils from the skin. Too much bathing will dry the coat and is an unnecessary stress on a puppy.

Grooming an Adult

Grooming your grown-up Cavalier three times a week is ideal under normal circumstances, but if you live in the country where there is long grass and burrs, you may need to do it more often.

Begin at the head and clean out the area at the inner corners of the eyes, which often have debris from "Cavalier tears." The tears can accumulate, dry out to a dark color and crusty texture, and be quite smelly. I keep cotton balls dampened with a tearstain solution for cleaning around the eyes. Be very careful not to get this solution anywhere near the eyes themselves, but only in the small area that is stained. Tear staining cannot be seen on Rubies and Black and Tans, but on Particolors who do not have much chestnut or black around the eye, tearstains will spoil the look of the face. Using tearstain formula whenever you are grooming may not completely eliminate the brownish color, but it will keep it under control.

Lift the ears and swab them with a makeup pad moistened with rubbing alcohol or commercial ear-cleaning solution. Never use a long cotton swab because of the danger of damaging the inner ear if the dog jerks his head. Some dogs become

Cavaliers may have problems with tear staining or matter in the corners of the eyes. Wipe them clean with a damp cotton ball.

very upset because of the strong smell of rubbing alcohol. If that's the case, you can substitute a small amount of baby oil.

Hold the mouth shut gently with one hand, and with the other insert a small toothbrush inside the cheek and brush the upper and lower back teeth with dog toothpaste. Now pull up the lip on one side and brush the upper side and front teeth and repeat the process on the other side.

Next, spray the outsides of the ears liberally with grooming spray (cupping your hand around the eye to protect it from the spray), then continue down the body, over the legs and tail, working the spray into the coat with your hands.

The comb and pin brush are next, working from the ears back, combing first and brushing second. Pay special attention to the area at the back of the ears. The hair there is extremely fine and knots easily. When using the pin brush it is best to do a small section at a time, first brushing against the lie of the hair down to the skin, then brushing with the natural lie of the hair to smooth it.

There may be tangles in the ear, leg or tail feathers that will not come out, and this is where the slicker brush comes into play. Hold the hair close to the skin with one hand and work away from the body in long smooth strokes with the slicker brush. The slicker will make the hair lie flat in one direction, taking out small tangles as it moves. It is also effective to tease out the tangle with your fingers and then use the slicker brush.

A tool that is a wonderful aid at shedding time in the spring is the Mars Coat-King, a German-made hand tool specifically designed for pulling out dead hair. It has a wooden handle and a stainless steel head with 20 curved teeth to catch the fine hair of the undercoat. It may seem expensive, but it is a one-time purchase that will never have to be repeated.

A slicker brush will remove tangles.

A spayed or neutered adult Cavalier will need to have his coat thinned because it will grow much longer and thicker than that of an unneutered animal. Insert the thinning shears close to the skin, against the lay of the hair, and snip away, beginning at the neck and working your way down each side. Next, thin the profuse hair, or feathers, at the back of the legs and the tail. After using the thinning shears, a good combing will pull out the excess hair.

After grooming the coat, check the toenails to see if they need cutting. They should be cut once every two or three weeks. Don't put it off! Pet owners dislike cutting nails because they are afraid they will cut the quick and hurt the dog. It is essential, however, to keep those toenails short. One reason is that they will not cause so much damage to floors and rugs, but the other, more important reason is that they can grow so long that they curl over, cause the dog discomfort, and throw off the whole balance of the leg, causing strain.

Some dogs don't like having their feet handled and will make a fuss about it, crying as if in distress even before you start to work on the nails. Be patient but insist on having your way. Take just the smallest clipping off each toenail to ensure that there will be absolutely no pain, and your dog will soon realize that this process is just part of normal grooming.

Creepy Crawlies

While you are brushing your dog, be sure to check his coat for signs of fleas, ticks, and other nasty little critters that may be hiding. Even dogs from the best of homes can end up with external parasites: They lurk in city parks, suburban lawns, and country lanes.

Fleas

Of all the external parasites, fleas are the most common cause of skin irritation for any dog. They hop onto the dog to ingest a blood meal, but they live and lay their eggs in the dog's environment. Fleas will live mainly on parts of the dog that he cannot reach by scratching, particularly on the lower back around the tail. If you see any little reddishblack flecks near the skin in this area, these are flea feces.

Acting upon the very first sign of a problem is the key to getting rid of fleas. When I suspect fleas, I bathe every dog, then comb through each one daily with a fine-tooth comb until the pesky critters are gone. Since I try to raise my Cavaliers in a natural way, I never use insecticides directly on my dogs, but instead use a spray for carpets, crates, and baseboards when I find signs of fleas

A fine-tooth comb will nicely finish off your dog's coat and is also a handy tool to check for fleas.

on my Cavaliers. The safest spray is one that uses natural pyrethrin, because it is least toxic to the dogs.

In the past few years, new and effective chemical treatments have been developed to combat fleas (see the box on page 79). Although flea baths and body sprays will temporarily rid your Cavalier of fleas, they will recur unless his room, bedding, carpets, and baseboards in the vicinity are treated (see the box on page 82).

If your dog is only bothered occasionally with a flea or two, the flea bath and treatment of the premises when necessary is the natural way to go, but if you live in a warm climate and fleas are a continuing problem, then the monthly treatments may be preferable. Some fleas can also carry tapeworm, and if your dog ingests an infected flea he will soon have his very own parasite (see chapter 8). This requires a trip to the veterinarian. For certain sensitive dogs, flea allergy dermatitis, appearing as crusted areas of skin with considerable loss of hair around the tail area, will be the result of only a few bites, and this condition will also require veterinary care.

Ticks

Check your dog for ticks every time you groom him. They must be removed with tweezers, and since the tick head is buried under the dog's skin, it must be done so that the head comes away with the tick's body (see the box on page 80).

New Products in the Fight Against Fleas

At one time, battling fleas meant exposing your dog and your-self to toxic dips, sprays, powders, and collars. But today there are flea preventives that work very well and are safe for your dog, you, and the environment. The two most common types are insect growth regulators (IGRs), which stop the immature flea from developing or maturing, and adult flea killers. To deal with an active infestation, experts usually recommend a product that has both.

These next-generation flea fighters generally come in one of two forms:

- **Topical treatments or spot-ons.** These products are applied to the skin, usually between the shoulder blades. The product is absorbed through the skin into the dog's system. Among the most widely available spot-ons are Advantage (kills adult fleas and larvae), Revolution (kills adult fleas), Frontline Plus (kills adult fleas and larvae, plus an IGR), K-9 Advantix (kills adult fleas and larvae), and BioSpot (kills adult fleas and larvae, plus an IGR).
- **Systemic products.** This is a pill your dog swallows that transmits a chemical throughout the dog's bloodstream. When a flea bites the dog, it picks up this chemical, which then prevents the flea's eggs from developing. Among the most widely available systemic products are Program (kills larvae only, plus an IGR) and Capstar (kills adult fleas).

Make sure you read all the labels and apply the products exactly as recommended, and that you check to be sure they are safe for puppies.

How to Get Rid of a Tick

During tick season (which, depending on where you live, can be spring, summer, and/or fall), examine your dog every day for ticks. Pay particular attention to your dog's neck, behind the ears, the armpits, and the groin.

When I find a tick, my method is to take a drop of pure tea tree oil and dab it on the tick. The shock will cause him to almost let go, then you can get a firm grip on the body with a pair of tweezers. Grasp the tick as close as possible to the dog's skin and pull it out using firm, steady pressure. Check to make sure you get the whole tick (mouth parts left in your dog's skin can cause an infection), then dab the wound with a little hydrogen peroxide and some antibiotic ointment. Watch for signs of inflammation.

Ticks carry very serious diseases that are transmittable to humans, so dispose of the tick safely. Never crush it between your fingers. Don't flush it down the toilet either, because the tick may survive the trip and infect another animal. Instead, use the tweezers to place the tick in a tight-sealing jar or plastic dish with a little alcohol, put on the lid and dispose of the container in an outdoor garbage can. Wash the tweezers thoroughly with hot water and rinse with alcohol.

A hazard to dogs and humans alike is the deer tick that can carry Lyme disease. Deer ticks are common in suburban and rural areas, especially in the northeast. If your dog picks up a tick and it is gray rather than brown, it is likely to be a deer tick. The first symptoms of Lyme disease are a rash that extends in a circle from the area of the bite. Following that first sign, the dog may exhibit fever, staggering, weakness, and subsequent swelling of the joints. Lyme disease can end in severe arthritis and heart problems.

Mites

There are several kinds of mites that can infest the skin. The most common among Cavaliers is the *Cheyletiella* mange mite, also known as "walking dandruff." *Cheyletiella* mites burrow into the skin to lay their eggs. There is intense itching of the skin and the dog will chew himself trying to get rid of the itch. When the mites hatch, a flake of skin comes off and this is the "dandruff" you can see. Apart from the apparent skin flakes, the coat will become thin and lose its luster. The mite itself cannot be seen with the naked eye, but can be detected with the veterinarian's microscope.

If the dog is itching and there is no apparent reason, a visit to the vet is in order to determine the cause. The vet will take a skin scraping from an area most likely to be affected to see if mites are present. The vet has several treatment options, depending on the severity and persistence of the infestation. These mites spend their lives on their host and generally do not get into the surrounding environment, as fleas do. It is a good idea, nevertheless, to change the dog's bedding if he has to be treated for mite infection.

Sarcoptic and demodectic mange also must be diagnosed by a professional and are more difficult to treat. At any sign of continual scratching, loss of hair around the eyes or lesions on the skin, the dog should be seen by the veterinarian without delay.

How to Bathe a Cavalier

Plan bath time for your Cavalier just after a grooming session. If you bathe him before grooming it can be a disaster, since any tangles or knots will be made much worse and it will be necessary to cut them out of the coat.

How often should you bathe your Cavalier? It depends on where you live and what the dog does. In the country there is clean air and the dirt, therefore, is "clean dirt" that brushes easily out of the coat. Regular grooming should be enough to keep the skin and coat in good condition. The occasional bath may be necessary if the dog has been out on a muddy day, for instance, and is just too dirty to bring into the house.

City living requires a regular regimen of bathing because of the pollution. City dirt is usually oily and particolors, in particular, get a gray tinge to the white of the coat, which is a sign that a bath is due.

Bathe your dog as often as is absolutely necessary, but no more than that. Too much bathing will strip the coat of its natural oils and will cause skin irritation.

The eyes and ears will need to be protected during the bath. A trace of petroleum jelly on the face around the eyes will keep soap and water from this sensitive area and cotton balls lightly coated with baby oil can be placed in the ears to prevent water from getting in and causing discomfort.

Although your Cavalier will happily plunge into a pool or lake, standing in the sink or tub and having a bath is a whole different kettle of dog. He may be

Making Your Environment Flea Free

If there are fleas on your dog, there are fleas in your home, yard, and car, even if you can't see them. Take these steps to combat them.

In your home:

- Wash whatever is washable (the dog bed, sheets, blankets, pillow covers, slipcovers, curtains, etc.).
- Vacuum everything else in your home—furniture, floors, rugs, everything. Pay special attention to the folds and crevices in upholstery, cracks between floorboards, and the spaces between the floor and the baseboards. Flea larvae are sensitive to sunlight, so inside the house they prefer deep carpet, bedding, and cracks and crevices.
- When you're done, throw the vacuum cleaner bag away—in an outside garbage can.
- Use a nontoxic flea-killing powder, such as Flea Busters or Zodiac FleaTrol, to treat your carpets (but remember, it does not control fleas elsewhere in the house). The powder stays deep in the carpet and kills fleas (using a form of boric acid) for up to a year.
- If you have a particularly serious flea problem, consider using a fogger or long-lasting spray to kill any adult and larval fleas, or having a professional exterminator treat your home.

nervous about being high up off the floor for a length of time, or he may be upset at being sprayed from head to toe. You may like the fragrance of the shampoo you are using but he may find it strange or unpleasant.

Talk to him reassuringly from the time you put him in the tub until he is lifted out, telling him what you are going to do next. He won't know what you are saying, but your tone of voice and your gentle movements, using as little restraint as possible, will make him feel less tense. The whole idea is to make the bathing process as pleasant as you can so that your Cavalier will be happy when the shampoo bottle comes out.

Put a small amount of the shampoo you have chosen into a plastic jug and fill the jug with lukewarm water to dilute it. Using water only, of the same barely warm temperature, wet the dog thoroughly from front to back. Wet hair will absorb the shampoo more readily. Don't use any shampoo from the ears forward, but use a cloth with only water on it to wipe the face, paying particular attention to the areas under the eyes and the upper and lower lips, which sometimes can accumulate debris.

In your car:

- Take out the floor mats and hose them down with a strong stream of water, then hang them up to dry in the sun.
- Wash any towels, blankets, or other bedding you regularly keep in the car.
- Thoroughly vacuum the entire interior of your car, paying special attention to the seams between the bottom and back of the seats.
- When you're done, throw the vacuum cleaner bag away—in an outside garbage can.

In your yard:

- Flea larvae prefer shaded areas that have plenty of organic material and moisture, so rake the yard thoroughly and bag all the debris in tightly sealed bags.
- Spray your yard with an insecticide that has residual activity for at least thirty days. Insecticides that use a form of boric acid are non-toxic. Some newer products contain an insect growth regulator (such as fenoxycarb) and need to be applied only once or twice a year.
- For an especially difficult flea problem, consider having an exterminator treat your yard.
- Keep your yard free of piles of leaves, weeds, and other organic debris. Be especially careful in shady, moist areas, such as under bushes.

Now take the diluted shampoo and, beginning at the ears, work your way back along the dog's body, not forgetting to lather under the body and the legs and feet. Rinse off the shampoo until the hair feels squeaky. At this point you can squeeze the excess water from the coat and apply a diluted conditioner, about a tablespoon to two quarts of water. It is safe to leave this in the coat. I prefer to towel dry my dogs and then use a grooming spray instead of a conditioner, but both methods work well.

Drying the coat can be as simple or as elaborate as you want to make it. After towel drying, run a comb through the damp coat and feathering to reveal any knots that have gone undetected. If you do not require a glamorous show finish and if the weather is warm and sunny, allow your dog to finish drying by running in the yard. On release from the bathtub into the yard your Cavalier will shake and race around madly, rolling in the grass and generally telling you how delighted he is to be free of such an unnatural procedure as a bath.

If you want to have a more professional finish on your dog's coat, or if it is just too cold to let your dog outside to air dry, a handheld hair dryer is the best

How often you bathe your dog depends on how dirty he gets.

tool to use. In any case, don't leave a damp dog to dry by himself in the house. He will take a long time to dry properly in these circumstances and may get a chill. The ears, in particular, because the hair is fine and thick, can take almost a whole day to dry naturally and thus are liable to bacterial infections such as canker, which thrives in a warm, damp atmosphere.

When using a dryer, put it on high volume but low heat. Cavaliers are very sensitive to temperature, and a hot dryer would be painful for the skin. Begin at the ears and use the pin brush to smooth the hair as you dry. When the dog is totally dry, use the bristle brush from head to toe to give a silky finish to the coat. Have some special treat ready as a reward, and give it to the dog as soon as you have finished brushing and while he is still on the table.

Now is the time to get out your camera to take a picture of your beautiful Cavalier. One run around the yard and one scratch of the ear will soon return your dog to slightly shaggy, less than perfect looks, but you will have the satisfaction of knowing that he is really clean from head to toe and that the thorough brushing you gave his skin and coat will be of great benefit to his general health.

Chapter 8

Keeping Your Cavalier Healthy

From the moment you come home with your new puppy, you are responsible for ensuring that everything is done to keep him in top condition. If you have been able to find a veterinarian who sees other Cavaliers (ask your puppy's breeder for a referral), it will be an advantage because there are specific health concerns for Cavaliers.

Your first visit to the vet should be simply to accustom your puppy to the clinic at a time when no treatment is necessary. At the same time, you can inquire about the schedule of fees for services so that you won't have any unpleasant surprises when it's time to pay the bill. While veterinarians are busy professionals, they should be willing to take time to answer any questions you have and explain about any course of treatment being considered.

Keep a calendar with the date of your puppy's first vaccination (which was given by the breeder) and make an appointment with your veterinarian for twenty-eight days from that date for a second booster. Show your veterinarian the first vaccination certificate so they will know what shots the puppy has had. Take with you any records of deworming or other health treatments, as well.

At the end of your visit your veterinarian will suggest a schedule of further vaccinations. You should be provided with a chart that shows your puppy's record of treatment, which you should then bring back on successive visits to be updated.

Vaccines

What vaccines dogs need and how often they need them has been a subject of controversy for several years. Researchers, health care professionals, vaccine manufacturers, and dog owners do not always agree on which vaccines each dog needs or how often booster shots must be given.

In 2003, the American Animal Hospital Association released vaccination guidelines and recommendations that have helped dog owners and veterinarians sort through much of the controversy and conflicting information. The guidelines designate four vaccines as core, or essential, because of the serious nature of the diseases and their widespread distribution. These are canine distemper virus, canine parvovirus, canine adenovirus-2, and rabies. The general recommendations for their use (except rabies, for which you must follow local laws) are:

- Vaccinate puppies at 6–8 weeks, 9–11 weeks, and 12–14 weeks.
- Give a booster shot when the dog is 1 year old.

Teething

At the age of 4 months your puppy may go off her food quite drastically. Maybe she has been a wonderful eater until this time and so you cannot help but be worried. The likely explanation is that she is teething and that her mouth is just plain sore. You can consider giving her soft food for a few weeks until the new teeth are in and her mouth is back to normal. Be sure to give her plenty of appropriate chew toys, as well.

Puppies usually return to hearty eating once the adult teeth are established. If a loss of appetite persists for more than a week or two, other causes must be sought with the help of your veterinarian.

Make sure that when her large upper incisors come in that they push out the baby teeth. Cavaliers are notorious for retaining these baby teeth, and if they

- Give a subsequent booster shot every three years, unless there are risk factors that make it necessary to vaccinate more or less often.

Noncore vaccines should only be considered for those dogs who risk exposure to a particular disease because of geographic area, lifestyle, frequency of travel, or other issues. They include vaccines against distemper-measles virus, canine parainfluenza virus, leptospirosis, Bordetella bronchiseptica, and Borrelia burgdorferi (Lyme disease).

Vaccines that are not generally recommended because the disease poses little risk to dogs or is easily treatable, or the vaccine has not been proven to be effective, are those against Giardia, canine coronavirus, and canine adenovirus-1.

Often, combination injections are given to puppies, with one shot containing several core and noncore vaccines. Your veterinarian may be reluctant to use separate shots that do not include the noncore vaccines, because they must be specially ordered. If you are concerned about these noncore vaccines, talk to your vet.

remain for too long they may decay and infect the permanent teeth. If you notice that the permanent teeth are in and the baby teeth are still there as well, you can try wiggling the baby teeth and this action may be enough to make them come out. If they are still tight the solution is to take the puppy to the vet to have the baby teeth removed. It is a simple procedure and does not need anesthesia.

Hereditary Diseases

The Cavalier is generally a sturdy, healthy dog, but there are genetic tendencies in the breed to develop certain health problems. All dogs are subject to inheritable diseases, and the Cavalier is no better or worse than other breeds.

Teething puppies may lose their appetite.

Here follows a list and description of the genetic diseases that can appear in Cavaliers. These conditions may occur in an occasional individual, even if the breeder has put heart and soul into the effort to find healthy lines and produce long-lived puppies. Although ethical breeders inform prospective pet owners about these diseases, there should not be too much emphasis put on them. Reputable breeders put much time, money, and effort into breeding away from inherited disease in their animals, and most will offer the buyer a one-year guarantee from date of birth against any disabling genetic defect.

Mitral Valve Disease

Mitral valve disease is the most serious of the inherited diseases affecting the breed. At the onset of this disease the left mitral valve of the heart begins to degenerate and leak, allowing small amounts of blood to flow the wrong way, causing strain on the heart. As the leak progresses, the heart must work harder to pump blood and becomes enlarged. From this point, the dog can go into congestive heart failure.

Mitral valve disease is seldom detected before a dog is one year old, and it usually comes to light when the dog goes for an annual checkup. The vet will hear a murmur through the stethoscope, although there may be no physical symptoms of heart trouble. A Cavalier may continue on with this slight murmur for many years, and the leak may progress so slowly that she remains without symptoms until she is quite old, when degeneration would be expected in any case. In some cases, however, a murmur will be detected and the dog will go downhill rapidly, progressing to congestive heart failure at the relatively early age of 7 or 8.

A Swedish study of mitral valve disease reveals that more than 50 percent of Cavaliers have a murmur detectable by stethoscope by the

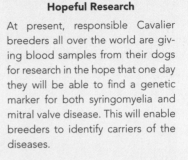

Hopeful Research

At present, responsible Cavalier breeders all over the world are giving blood samples from their dogs for research in the hope that one day they will be able to find a genetic marker for both syringomyelia and mitral valve disease. This will enable breeders to identify carriers of the diseases.

time they are 4 years old. The normal life span of a Cavalier is 10 to 12 years, and it is the aim of breeders to try to produce puppies who will be healthy and long-lived.

Environmental factors play a part in the progression of mitral valve disease. A dog who is fat and gets little exercise is a prime candidate for the problem. Keeping a Cavalier slim and active will give her the best chance to cope if she is diagnosed with mitral valve disease. My first Cavalier, Ollie, who lived to be nearly 15, developed mitral valve disease at age 6 and was symptom free until he was more than 12 years old. I ascribe his remarkable longevity entirely to his strong constitution, good nutrition, and the fact that he trotted a mile or two every day of his life.

The diagnosis of mitral valve disease is not a death sentence, and there are a number of helpful drugs that will improve the quality of life for an affected dog. Drugs are usually prescribed when the dog begins to exhibit symptoms such as shortness of breath or coughing. These can be alleviated with one or a combination of drugs, depending upon which symptoms are present. Veterinarians can supply prescription diets for dogs who have mitral valve disease; these are usually fairly low in protein with no salt added.

Patella Luxation

Patella luxation is an orthopedic problem in which the kneecap (patella) slips out of its groove at the front of the thighbone. This can occur because the groove is too shallow—an inherited problem. An accident or heavy blow at the side of the knee can also displace the patella. In the case of an accident, once this has occurred the kneecap is more likely to be displaced again.

If you see unexplained occasional limping, or if your dog stops now and again to stretch out the affected leg (which causes the kneecap to go back into

Knee problems can be corrected if they are caught early.

place), it is possible your dog has a luxating patella. It is easy for veterinarians to diagnose this condition by manipulating the leg to see if there is sideways movement of the patella.

Veterinary orthopedic surgeons have devised a highly successful operation to correct patella luxation. It consists of deepening the groove in the femur so that the kneecap will not slip out. The symptoms of this condition may be noticed while the dog is still a puppy, and the sooner the operation can be done, the better the results. Later in life the dog may have some arthritis as a result of the operation, but that is better than life with a knee that is crippling and painful.

Reputable breeders will test their potential sires and dams and clear them of patella luxation before breeding. Producing dogs with good, solid bone structure is a first step to correcting the problem. Dogs with delicate legs are much more prone to this kind of problem, and in any case, a "chicken-boned" Cavalier is not a pretty sight.

Hip Dysplasia

The hip is a ball and socket joint. In normal hips the ball fits very closely into a nicely rounded socket. In dogs with hip dysplasia the socket begins to flatten out and the ball of the head of the femur no longer fits tightly. Laxity in the joint causes more wear and tear on the socket, which will eventually grow bone spurs, causing a lot of pain for the dog.

While hip dysplasia can occur in Cavaliers, it is relatively rare when compared to patella luxation. Dysplasia is much more of a problem in large breeds, because the bones of large breed puppies grow much more rapidly in a very short time.

Symptoms of this problem include difficulty in rising after being in one position for some time, leaning forward when sitting to take the weight of the body on the front legs, and "bunny hopping" with the back legs rather than trotting. A dog may have hip dysplasia and yet show no signs for some years. It is only when the disease is quite advanced that you may notice limping or the symptoms mentioned here.

Anti-inflammatory drugs and painkillers can be prescribed by your vet for a mild condition. If it becomes severe, an orthopedic surgeon can perform an operation, but this usually requires a long convalescence and is very expensive.

Retinal Dysplasia

The retina of the eye may be compared to a shallow, smooth, round bowl. In a dog with dysplasia, the surface of the "bowl" has wrinkles or folds. In a mild case of retinal dysplasia there will be only a few folds, and this is known as the focal type. Where there are many folds, the condition is known as the geographic type.

No one can tell you how the dog's sight is affected, and in my experience the dog does not seem to suffer at all from any disability from either grade of retinal dysplasia.

If you have a pet Cavalier with retinal dysplasia you may never find out about it. Breeders, however, are very concerned and strive not to knowingly breed this condition into their puppies. That's because in other breeds, retinal dysplasia has progressed to such a point that dogs suffer retinal detachment and go blind. (At the present time any grade of retinal detachment in the Cavalier has never progressed or proceeded to blindness.)

Cataracts

Cataracts are not widespread in the Cavalier, and they may be hereditary or congenital (present from the time of birth). In the congenital type, they remain static and do not progress to blindness. Cataracts that develop later in life do progress, and the end result is blindness, although usually at an advanced age.

Old-age cataracts are common in all breeds. Dogs so affected can still lead fairly normal lives if they are living in a known environment where they are familiar with the physical layout of home and yard.

Epilepsy

Epilepsy can occur in Cavaliers, but it is also not common. The term covers all kinds of seizures, and it is difficult if not impossible for a veterinarian to determine if epileptic seizures are the result of an accident as a puppy or if they are inherited.

When a dog is having a seizure she will collapse, she may froth at the mouth or her jaw will clench, her legs will move involuntarily, and she may lose consciousness for a few seconds or even minutes. After the seizure is over, the dog will appear lethargic and when she gets up may seem uncoordinated for a while.

Hereditary epilepsy is uncommon in the Cavalier, but is known to occur. It usually begins when the dog is 6 months to a year old, appears without any warning, and apparently without any particular triggering event. One minute the dog will be walking happily on the leash and the next minute she's on the ground in the throes of a seizure. Fortunately, seizures can be controlled by drugs, and many dogs so afflicted can lead normal lives.

There is a condition related to epilepsy that may occur in Cavaliers, known as fly-catching syndrome. The dog looks around and seems to be snapping at nonexistent flies. Medication is not needed for this condition, since the dog is not disabled in any way. But if it becomes excessive, the same drugs that are used for epilepsy are effective for this problem.

Good breeding and good care will keep your dog fit throughout her life.

Syringomyelia

Syringomyelia is sometimes referred to as neck scratcher's disease because scratching in the air near the neck is a common sign. The condition is caused by slowing of the flow of cerebro-spinal fluid because the back of the brain is extending downward and obstructing the top of the spinal column.

Progression of the disease is very variable. Some dogs have happy and long lives with minor symptoms and without significant deterioration until old age. Others may progress to pain and muscle weakness earlier on. There is an operation that can be performed to alleviate the condition, but it is delicate, expensive, has a long recovery process, and does not always work.

Do not panic if your dog scratches. She may just have a temporary itch, a fly bite, or even a flea.

No one can see into the future and absolutely guarantee a healthy dog. But responsible breeders test their dogs for hereditary defects, understand the complex genetics of breeding, and do their best to produce sound dogs.

It is the habit of scratching hard and crying, or habitually walking and scratching at the same time, that will give you a clue that the dog needs to be examined by a veterinarian. An MRI is the only way to determine if a dog does have syringomyelia.

An Innocent Anomaly

There is a condition unique to the Cavalier that involves blood platelet count. If your Cavalier has to have a blood test for any reason, your veterinarian may be alarmed by the large size and small number of your dog's blood platelets. Many veterinarians are not familiar with Cavaliers, and will consider investigating to discover whether the dog has a condition known as thrombocytopenia. If your Cavalier appears to be healthy and has no other symptoms of illness, then your veterinarian should be informed that Cavaliers carry this trait of large blood platelets as an autosomal recessive, and that it is perfectly normal in this breed.

Common Canine Ailments

Tooth Decay

Gingivitis and tooth decay are common ailments of the Cavalier. The muzzle is relatively short compared to that of a German Shepherd, for instance, but they both have the same number of teeth. Consequently, the Cavalier's teeth are packed closely together. Brushing daily with a baby toothbrush and toothpaste made specifically for dogs (see chapter 7) is the best way to avoid infection. As mentioned in chapter 7, the bacteria resulting from gingivitis can travel through the bloodstream to the valves of the heart and weaken them.

Internal Parasites

For pets who are cared for regularly by a veterinarian, internal parasites are no longer the threat they once were. Regular stool examinations as part of a routine checkup will identify most problems, and then proper treatment can be prescribed. With the exception of heartworms, internal parasites are not difficult to eliminate with the right medicine. Cavaliers who live in the country with all kinds of wildlife that can transmit parasites need to be watched carefully for poor condition of coat, lethargy, and haggard appearance that would indicate worms.

Never buy over-the-counter worm remedies that are for sale in the pet supply store or the supermarket. The medication may be incorrect for the type of worm the dog has, in which case it will not solve the problem, and you will have given your dog unnecessary medication. Taking a stool sample to your veterinarian for analysis once every six months is good insurance against worms of any kind. The vet will give you the correct medication for whatever parasite your dog has picked up.

Many canine parasites are zoonotic, which means they can be passed to humans. Children tend to be more susceptable—another good reason to keep your dog healthy and parasite-free.

Heartworm

Heartworms are carried by an intermediate host, the mosquito. It bites an infected dog and ingests heartworm microfilariae (the immature stage of parasite), which are present in the dog's blood. When the mosquito bites another dog, a little of the infected blood is introduced and the heartworm lifecycle begins. If the infection goes undetected, these microfilariae will develop into large adult worms that will clog the heart, and death is the end result.

Heartworm is much easier to prevent than it is to cure. A pill given once a month will kill any microfilariae in the blood. Medication for prevention of heartworm is essential in nearly all areas of the United States. Heartworm preventives will also eliminate all the other types of internal parasites except tapeworms.

A dog who is already infested with adult worms can be treated with drugs that are basically poisons, but even if the worms are dislodged by chemical means, the dog's heart will be weakened for life.

Anal Glands

Anal glands are located on each side of the anus, and they secrete a substance that enables your dog to pass her stool. When they become clogged, they are extremely uncomfortable, smell bad, and could get infected. I have commented on the breed trait of "scooting" in chapter 3. Even young puppies will exhibit this

If your dog suddenly seems less active than normal, it's time to visit the vet.

When to Call the Veterinarian

Go to the vet right away or take your dog to an emergency veterinary clinic if:

- Your dog is choking.
- Your dog is having trouble breathing.
- Your dog has been injured and you cannot stop the bleeding within a few minutes.
- Your dog has been stung or bitten by an insect and the site is swelling.
- Your dog has been bitten by a snake.
- Your dog has been bitten by another animal (including a dog) and shows any swelling or bleeding.
- Your dog has touched, licked, or in any way been exposed to a poison.
- Your dog has been burned by either heat or caustic chemicals.
- Your dog has been hit by a car.
- Your dog has any obvious broken bones or cannot put any weight on one of her limbs.
- Your dog has a seizure.

behavior occasionally. The difference between this habit and scooting because the anal glands are full or impacted is in the frequency with which it occurs.

Your veterinarian can quickly unclog the anal glands, or you can do it yourself if you are game. Just use one hand to hold the tail up and, with a tissue or soft cloth in your other hand, take the skin on either side of the anus, just below the middle, in your thumb and forefinger. Then push in slightly and squeeze gently. If you succeed, a brownish, nasty-smelling substance will be on your cloth and your Cavalier will stop scooting.

Blood or pus in the secretion is a sign of infection, so if either one is present, take your dog to the veterinarian.

Make an appointment to see the vet as soon as possible if:

- Your dog has been bitten by a cat, another dog, or a wild animal.
- Your dog has been injured and is still limping an hour later.
- Your dog has unexplained swelling or redness.
- Your dog's appetite changes.
- Your dog vomits repeatedly and can't seem to keep food down, or drools excessively while eating.
- You see any changes in your dog's urination or defecation (pain during elimination, change in regular habits, blood in urine or stool, diarrhea, foul-smelling stool).
- Your dog continually scoots her rear end on the floor.
- Your dog's energy level, attitude, or behavior changes for no apparent reason.
- Your dog has crusty or cloudy eyes, or excessive tearing or discharge.
- Your dog's nose is dry or chapped, hot, crusty, or runny.
- Your dog's ears smell foul, have a dark discharge, or seem excessively waxy.
- Your dog's gums are inflamed or bleeding, her teeth look brown, or her breath is foul.
- Your dog's skin is red, flaky, itchy, or inflamed, or she keeps chewing at certain spots.
- Your dog's coat is dull, dry, brittle, or bare in spots.
- Your dog's paws are red, swollen, tender, cracked, or the nails are split or too long.
- Your dog is panting excessively, wheezing, unable to catch her breath, breathing heavily, or sounds strange when she breathes.

Vomiting

Vomiting is a natural reaction when a dog's stomach is irritated for any reason. In fact, dogs will deliberately go out and eat types of coarse grass that will cause vomiting. The time to be concerned about vomiting is if the dog vomits her meals regularly or if the vomit has a foul odor or it contains blood. Another reason for being concerned is that continued vomiting may indicate a blockage of the bowel. In these cases, a visit to the veterinarian is in order to determine the cause of the problem.

Common Diarrhea

Cavaliers may get stomach upsets from a change of food, a change of water when traveling, or because they have picked up something tainted from the ground and swallowed it. As long as the diarrhea is not bloody and foul and stops within a few hours, there should be no more problems. Diarrhea that continues past this time may be more serious and should be treated by a veterinarian.

What to Do in an Emergency

Dog Bites

A Cavalier is a sociable soul, and if not watched she will run happily to any person with a dog in the park to make their acquaintance. Trouble can often result when the other dog takes exception to this carefree visitor and bites her. These are usually puncture wounds.

To treat them, first press on the puncture wound from underneath the area so that it will bleed a little to expel bacteria that may have got into the wound with the teeth. Next, using a cotton pad, soak the wound well with hydrogen peroxide. Then cover it with a clean bandage. A visit to the veterinarian within twelve to twenty-four hours is in order so that he can prescribe an antibiotic to avoid any infection. Puncture wounds may swell and be painful but they seldom need stitches.

In a more serious bite, there may be a tear in the skin as well as puncture wounds. If there is considerable bleeding, apply pressure to the wound with your hand to slow the blood flow. Flush the wound as soon as you can with hydrogen peroxide and go to a veterinarian right away, because stitches may be necessary.

Choking

All kinds of objects can get stuck in your dog's throat—small balls, sticks, or pieces of soft plastic toys, for example. Symptoms of choking are gagging and coughing as the dog tries to dislodge the object, and she will be frantic. If you have another person handy, get them to hold the dog still. Open the dog's mouth to see if you can see the object and hook it out with your finger. If you cannot hook it out, hold the dog slanting downward and hit her sharply between the shoulders near the neck to see if the object will pop out. If this does not work, you can try laying the dog on her side and compressing sharply just behind the ribs. The hope is that air will be forced out of the lungs, and the object with it. If none of this works, it's an emergency and you must get your dog to the vet immediately.

How to Make a Canine First-Aid Kit

If your dog hurts herself, even a minor cut, it can be very upsetting for both of you. Having a first-aid kit handy will help you to help her, calmly and efficiently. What should be in your canine first-aid kit?

- Antibiotic ointment
- Antiseptic and antibacterial cleansing wipes
- Benadryl
- Cotton-tipped applicators
- Disposable razor
- Elastic wrap bandages
- Extra leash and collar
- First-aid tape of various widths
- Gauze bandage roll
- Gauze pads of different sizes, including eye pads
- Hydrogen peroxide
- Instant cold compress
- Kaopectate tablets or liquid
- Latex gloves
- Lubricating jelly
- Muzzle
- Nail clippers
- Pen, pencil, and paper for notes and directions
- Pepto-Bismol
- Round-ended scissors and pointy scissors
- Safety pins
- Sterile saline eyewash
- Thermometer (rectal)
- Tweezers

Heatstroke

The most common cause of heatstroke is leaving a dog in a car in warm weather. The symptoms of heatstroke are rapid panting, thick, bubbling saliva, staggering, and collapse. Wet the dog thoroughly as soon as you possibly can, or put her in a bath of cool water. Don't use ice in the water because it is too much of a shock to the system. She may be too weak to drink voluntarily, but you can squirt small amounts of water from a syringe (without the needle) down her throat at frequent intervals. She may be quite weak afterward from the shock to her system. Dry her well with a towel, wrap her in a blanket, and keep her in a cool place for the next few hours.

Hypothermia

It is less usual for a Cavalier to suffer from hypothermia, but it can happen as a result of being in very cold water or being outside in a northern winter too long without physical activity to keep the body warm. Symptoms of hypothermia include violent shivering, a belly that will feel cold to the touch, and a dog who will only be able to move very slowly.

If she is wet, dry her off as best you can. Wrap her in a towel and cuddle her next to your own body underneath your shirt or sweater. If she is dry, you can just put her under the sweater to begin warming. The best treatment for hypothermia is gradual, not quick, warming, and your body heat will do it nicely until you can get the dog indoors. Once inside, wrap her in a blanket to conserve her own body heat and put her in her own bed. Place large plastic soda pop bottles filled with warm water on each side of her and replenish as needed.

A young dog or an old one may need protection from the cold.

In an emergency, your dog will rely on you to be calm and know what to do.

Electric Shock

Puppies are particularly vulnerable to this type of injury because they want to find out about the world with their teeth. Electrical outlets in the home are usually near the floor and lamps are always left plugged in. A chewing puppy can get a serious shock if she is not discovered before her teeth contact the live wire in the cord, and the shock can be so severe that she can die. If she is not breathing, try artificial respiration, as described in the following section. Wrap her warmly and take her directly to the veterinarian.

Artificial Respiration

Clamp your hand around the dog's muzzle so no air can leak out. Inhale. Completely cover her nose with your mouth and exhale gently every five or six seconds, or ten to twelve breaths per minute, making sure her chest expands on every breath. Between each breath, remove your mouth from her nose until her chest deflates.

Note: *Even in respiratory arrest, a dog can close her jaws by reflex, without warning; be careful with your face so close to hers.* Call your veterinarian as soon as possible.

Even these hardy spaniels can drown. If you plan to take your Cavalier boating, get her a life jacket.

Severe Injury

After an accident, your first concern should be to stop the bleeding as much as possible, and your second concern is to get the dog to a veterinary hospital.

Start by applying direct pressure on the wound, using the cleanest cloth you have available or even your hand. If this doesn't work, bleeding from a limb can be slowed in an emergency by using a tourniquet above the wound. A belt or a tie can be used for this purpose, but the tourniquet must be loosened every ten minutes to keep the circulation in the limb going.

If the dog is conscious and snapping because of pain, a muzzle can be made out of a tie, a scarf, or a belt. Wind it around the dog's muzzle and then around the back of the head and secure it. To transport the dog for veterinary help, don't pick her up by the body. Roll her into some sort of sling—your jacket or a blanket, for instance—pull it taut, and carry her as on a stretcher.

ASPCA Animal Poison Control Center

The ASPCA Animal Poison Control Center has a staff of licensed veterinarians and board-certified toxicologists available 24 hours a day, 365 days a year. The number to call is (888) 426-4435. You will be charged a consultation fee of $50 per case, charged to most major credit cards. There is no charge for follow-up calls in critical cases. At your request, they will also contact your veterinarian. Specific treatment and information can be provided via fax. Put the number in large, legible print with your other emergency telephone numbers. Be prepared to give your name, address, and phone number; what your dog has gotten into (the amount and how long ago); your dog's breed, age, sex, and weight; and what signs and symptoms the dog is showing. You can log onto www.aspca.org and click on "Animal Poison Control Center" for more information, including a list of toxic and nontoxic plants.

Poisons

Common poisons around the home and yard include antifreeze, chocolate, cleaning solvents, disinfectants, houseplants, insecticides, slug bait, mouse or rat poison, pine oil cleaners, soaps, and detergents. Symptoms of poisoning include vomiting, convulsions, lack of coordination, and collapse. If you suspect poisoning, get to the veterinarian as quickly as possible because some poisons are fast acting.

Part III

Enjoying Your Cavalier King Charles Spaniel

Chapter 9

Training Your Cavalier

by Peggy Moran

Training makes your best friend better! A properly trained dog has a happier life and a longer life expectancy. He is also more appreciated by the people he encounters each day, both at home and out and about.

A trained dog walks nicely and joins his family often, going places untrained dogs cannot go. He is never rude or unruly, and he always happily comes when called. When he meets people for the first time, he greets them by sitting and waiting to be petted, rather than jumping up. At home he doesn't compete with his human family, and alone he is not destructive or overly anxious. He isn't continually nagged with words like "no," since he has learned not to misbehave in the first place. He is never shamed, harshly punished, or treated unkindly, and he is a well-loved, involved member of the family.

Sounds good, doesn't it? If you are willing to invest some time, thought, and patience, the words above could soon be used to describe your dog (though perhaps changing "he" to "she"). Educating your pet in a positive way is fun and easy, and there is no better gift you can give your pet than the guarantee of improved understanding and a great relationship.

This chapter will explain how to offer kind leadership, reshape your pet's behavior in a positive and practical way, and even get a head start on simple obedience training.

Understanding Builds the Bond

Dog training is a learning adventure on both ends of the leash. Before attempting to teach their dog new behaviors or change unwanted ones, thoughtful dog owners take the time to understand why their pets behave the way they do, and how their own behavior can be either a positive or negative influence on their dog.

Canine Nature

Loving dogs as much as we do, it's easy to forget they are a completely different species. Despite sharing our homes and living as appreciated members of our families, dogs do not think or learn exactly the same way people do. Even if you love your dog like a child, you must remember to respect the fact that he is actually a dog.

Dogs have no idea when their behavior is inappropriate from a human perspective. They are not aware of the value of possessions they chew or of messes they make or the worry they sometimes seem to cause. While people tend to look at behavior as good and bad or right and wrong, dogs just discover what works and what doesn't work. Then they behave accordingly, learning from their own experiences and increasing or reducing behaviors to improve results for themselves.

You might wonder, "But don't dogs want to please us"? My answer is yes, provided your pleasure reflects back to them in positive ways they can feel and appreciate. Dogs do things for *dog* reasons, and everything they do works for them in some way or they wouldn't be doing it!

The Social Dog

Our pets descended from animals who lived in tightly knit, cooperative social groups. Though far removed in appearance and lifestyle from their ancestors, our dogs still relate in many of the same ways their wild relatives did. And in their relationships with one another, wild canids either lead or follow.

Canine ranking relationships are not about cruelty and power; they are about achievement and abilities. Competent dogs with high levels of drive and confidence step up, while deferring dogs step aside. But followers don't get the short end of the stick; they benefit from the security of having a more competent dog at the helm.

Our domestic dogs still measure themselves against other members of their group—us! Dog owners whose actions lead to positive results have willing, secure followers. But dogs may step up and fill the void or cut loose and do their own thing when their people fail to show capable leadership. When dogs are pushy, aggressive, and rude, or independent and unwilling, it's not because they have designs on the role of "master." It is more likely their owners failed to provide consistent leadership.

Dogs in training benefit from their handler's good leadership. Their education flows smoothly because they are impressed. Being in charge doesn't require you to physically dominate or punish your dog. You simply need to make some subtle changes in the way you relate to him every day.

Lead Your Pack!

Create schedules and structure daily activities. Dogs are creatures of habit and routines will create security. Feed meals at the same times each day and also try to schedule regular walks, training practices, and toilet outings. Your predictability will help your dog be patient.

Ask your dog to perform a task. Before releasing him to food or freedom, have him do something as simple as sit on command. Teach him that cooperation earns great results!

Give a release prompt (such as "let's go") when going through doors leading outside. This is a better idea than allowing your impatient pup to rush past you.

Pet your dog when he is calm, not when he is excited. Turn your touch into a tool that relaxes and settles.

Reward desirable rather than inappropriate behavior. Petting a jumping dog (who hasn't been invited up) reinforces jumping. Pet sitting dogs, and only invite lap dogs up after they've first "asked" by waiting for your invitation.

Replace personal punishment with positive reinforcement. Show a dog what *to do,* and motivate him to want to do it, and there will be no need to punish him for what he should *not do.* Dogs naturally follow, without the need for force or harshness.

Play creatively and appropriately. Your dog will learn the most about his social rank when he is playing with you. During play, dogs work to control toys and try to get the best of one another in a friendly way. The wrong sorts of play can create problems: For example, tug of war can lead to aggressiveness. Allowing your dog to control toys during play may result in possessive guarding when he has something he really values, such as a bone. Dogs who are chased during play may later run away from you when you approach to leash them. The right kinds of play will help increase your dog's social confidence while you gently assert your leadership.

How Dogs Learn (and How They Don't)

Dog training begins as a meeting of minds—yours and your dog's. Though the end goal may be to get your dog's body to behave in a specific way, training starts as a mind game. Your dog is learning all the time by observing the consequences of his actions and social interactions. He is always seeking out what he perceives as desirable and trying to avoid what he perceives as undesirable.

He will naturally repeat a behavior that either brings him more good stuff or makes bad stuff go away (these are both types of reinforcement). He will naturally avoid a behavior that brings him more bad stuff or makes the good stuff go away (these are both types of punishment).

Both reinforcement and punishment can be perceived as either the direct result of something the dog did himself, or as coming from an outside source.

Using Life's Rewards

Your best friend is smart and he is also cooperative. When the best things in life can only be had by working with you, your dog will view you as a facilitator. You unlock doors to all of the positively reinforcing experiences he values: his freedom, his friends at the park, food, affection, walks, and play. The trained dog accompanies you through those doors and waits to see what working with you will bring.

Rewarding your dog for good behavior is called positive reinforcement, and, as we've just seen, it increases the likelihood that he will repeat that behavior. The perfect reward is anything your dog wants that is safe and appropriate. Don't limit yourself to toys, treats, and things that come directly from you. Harness life's positives—barking at squirrels, chasing a falling leaf, bounding away from you at the dog park, pausing for a moment to sniff everything—and allow your dog to earn access to those things as rewards that come from cooperating with you. When he looks at you, when he sits, when he comes when you call—any prompted behavior can earn one of life's rewards. When he works with you, he earns the things he most appreciates; but when he tries to get those things on his own, he cannot. Rather than seeing you as someone who always says "no," your dog will view you as the one who says "let's go!" He will *want* to follow.

What About Punishment?

Not only is it unnecessary to personally punish dogs, it is abusive. No matter how convinced you are that your dog "knows right from wrong," in reality he will associate personal punishment with the punisher. The resulting cowering, "guilty"-looking postures are actually displays of submission and fear. Later,

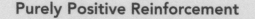

Purely Positive Reinforcement

With positive training, we emphasize teaching dogs what they should do to earn reinforcements, rather than punishing them for unwanted behaviors.

- Focus on teaching "do" rather than "don't." For example, a sitting dog isn't jumping.
- Use positive reinforcers that are valuable to your dog and the situation: A tired dog values rest; a confined dog values freedom.
- Play (appropriately)!
- Be a consistent leader.
- Set your dog up for success by anticipating and preventing problems.
- Notice and reward desirable behavior, and give him lots of attention when he is being good.
- Train ethically. Use humane methods and equipment that do not frighten or hurt your dog.
- When you are angry, walk away and plan a positive strategy.
- Keep practice sessions short and sweet. Five to ten minutes, three to five times a day is best.

when the punisher isn't around and the coast is clear, the same behavior he was punished for—such as raiding a trash can—might bring a self-delivered, very tasty result. The punished dog hasn't learned not to misbehave; he has learned to not get caught.

Does punishment ever have a place in dog training? Many people will heartily insist it does not. But dog owners often get frustrated as they try to stick to the path of all-positive reinforcement. It sure sounds great, but is it realistic, or even natural, to *never* say "no" to your dog?

A wild dog's life is not *all* positive. Hunger and thirst are both examples of negative reinforcement; the resulting discomfort motivates the wild dog to seek food and water. He encounters natural aversives such as pesky insects; mats in his coat; cold days; rainy days; sweltering hot days; and occasional run-ins with thorns, brambles, skunks, bees, and other nastiness. These all affect his behavior, as he tries to avoid the bad stuff whenever possible. The wild dog also occasionally encounters social punishers from others in his group when he gets too pushy. Starting with a growl or a snap from Mom, and later some mild and ritualized discipline from other members of his four-legged family, he learns to modify behaviors that elicit grouchy responses.

Our pet dogs don't naturally experience all positive results either, because they learn from their surroundings and from social experiences with other dogs. Watch a group of pet dogs playing together and you'll see a very old educational system still being used. As they wrestle and attempt to assert themselves, you'll notice many mouth-on-neck moments. Their playful biting is inhibited, with no intention to cause harm, but their message is clear: "Say uncle or this could hurt more!"

Observing that punishment does occur in nature, some people may feel compelled to try to be like the big wolf with their pet dogs. Becoming aggressive or heavy-handed with your pet will backfire! Your dog will not be impressed, nor will he want to follow you. Punishment causes dogs to change their behavior to avoid or escape discomfort and threats. Threatened dogs will either become very passive and offer submissive, appeasing postures, attempt to flee, or rise to the occasion and fight back. When people personally punish their dogs in an angry manner, one of these three defensive mechanisms will be triggered. Which one depends on a dog's genetic temperament as well as his past social experiences. Since we don't want to make our pets feel the need to avoid or escape us, personal punishment has no place in our training.

Remote Consequences

Sometimes, however, all-positive reinforcement is just not enough. That's because not all reinforcement comes from us. An inappropriate behavior can be self-reinforcing—just doing it makes the dog feel better in some way, whether you are there to say "good boy!" or not. Some examples are eating garbage, pulling the stuffing out of your sofa, barking at passersby, or urinating on the floor.

Although you don't want to personally punish your dog, the occasional deterrent may be called for to help derail these kinds of self-rewarding misbehaviors. In these cases, mild forms of impersonal or remote punishment can be used as part of a correction. The goal isn't to make your dog feel bad or to "know he has done wrong," but to help redirect him to alternate behaviors that are more acceptable to you.

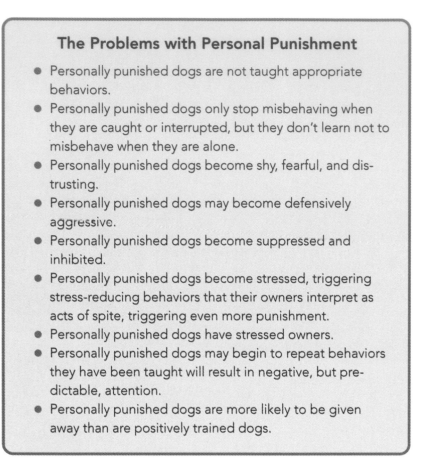

The Problems with Personal Punishment

- Personally punished dogs are not taught appropriate behaviors.
- Personally punished dogs only stop misbehaving when they are caught or interrupted, but they don't learn not to misbehave when they are alone.
- Personally punished dogs become shy, fearful, and distrusting.
- Personally punished dogs may become defensively aggressive.
- Personally punished dogs become suppressed and inhibited.
- Personally punished dogs become stressed, triggering stress-reducing behaviors that their owners interpret as acts of spite, triggering even more punishment.
- Personally punished dogs have stressed owners.
- Personally punished dogs may begin to repeat behaviors they have been taught will result in negative, but predictable, attention.
- Personally punished dogs are more likely to be given away than are positively trained dogs.

You do this by pairing a slightly startling, totally impersonal sound with an equally impersonal and *very mild* remote consequence. The impersonal sound might be a single shake of an empty plastic pop bottle with pennies in it, held out of your dog's sight. Or you could use a vocal expression such as "eh!" delivered with you looking *away* from your misbehaving dog.

Pair your chosen sound—the penny bottle or "eh!"—with either a slight tug on his collar or a sneaky spritz on the rump from a water bottle. Do this right *as* he touches something he should not; bad timing will confuse your dog and undermine your training success.

To keep things under your control and make sure you get the timing right, it's best to do this as a setup. "Accidentally" drop a shoe on the floor, and then help your dog learn some things are best avoided. As he sniffs the shoe say "eh!" without looking at him and give a *slight* tug against his collar. This sound will quickly become meaningful as a correction all by itself—sometimes after just one setup—making the tug correction obsolete. The tug lets your dog see that you were right; going for that shoe *was* a bad idea! Your wise dog will be more likely to heed your warning next time, and probably move closer to you where it's safe. Be a good friend and pick up the nasty shoe. He'll be relieved and you'll look heroic. Later, when he's home alone and encounters a stray shoe, he'll want to give it a wide berth.

Your negative marking sound will come in handy in the future, when your dog begins to venture down the wrong behavioral path. The goal is not to announce your disapproval or to threaten your dog. You are not telling him to stop or showing how *you* feel about his behavior. You are sounding a warning to a friend who's venturing off toward danger—"I wouldn't if I were you!" Suddenly, there is an abrupt, rather startling, noise! Now is the moment to redirect him and help him earn positive reinforcement. That interrupted behavior will become something he wants to avoid in the future, but he won't want to avoid you.

Practical Commands for Family Pets

Before you begin training your dog, let's look at some equipment you'll want to have on hand:

- **A buckle collar** is fine for most dogs. If your dog pulls *very* hard, try a head collar, a device similar to a horse halter that helps reduce pulling by turning the dog's head. *Do not* use a choke chain (sometimes called a training collar), because they cause physical harm even when used correctly.
- **Six-foot training leash and twenty-six–foot retractable leash.**
- **A few empty plastic soda bottles with about twenty pennies in each one.** This will be used to impersonally interrupt misbehaviors before redirecting dogs to more positive activities.
- **A favorite squeaky toy,** to motivate, attract attention, and reward your dog during training.

Baby Steps

Lure your dog to take just a few steps with you on the leash by being inviting and enthusiastic. Make sure you reward him for his efforts.

Allow your young pup to drag a short, lightweight leash attached to a buckle collar for a few *supervised* moments, several times each day. At first the leash may annoy him and he may jump around a bit trying to get away from it. Distract him with your squeaky toy or a bit of his kibble and he'll quickly get used to his new "tail."

Begin walking him on the leash by holding the end and following him. As he adapts, you can begin to assert gentle direct pressure to teach him to follow you. Don't jerk or yank, or he will become afraid to walk when the leash is on. If he becomes hesitant, squat down facing him and let him figure out that by moving toward you he is safe and secure. If he remains confused or frightened and doesn't come to you, go to him and help him understand that you provide safe harbor while he's on the leash. Then back away a few steps and try again to lure him to you. As he learns that you are the "home base," he'll want to follow when you walk a few steps, waiting for you to stop, squat down, and make him feel great.

So Attached to You!

The next step in training your dog—and this is a very important one—is to begin spending at least an hour or more each day with him on a four- to six-foot leash, held by or tethered to you. This training will increase his attachment to you—literally!—as you sit quietly or walk about, tending to your household business. When you are quiet, he'll learn it is time to settle; when you are active, he'll learn to move with you. Tethering also keeps him out of trouble when you are busy but still want his company. It is a great alternative to confining a dog, and can be used instead of crating any time you're home and need to slow him down a bit.

Rotating your dog from supervised freedom to tethered time to some quiet time in the crate or his gated area gives him a diverse and balanced day while he is learning. Two confined or tethered hours is the most you should require of your dog in one stretch, before changing to some supervised freedom, play, or a walk.

The dog in training may, at times, be stressed by all of the changes he is dealing with. Provide a stress outlet, such as a toy to chew on, when he is confined or tethered. He will settle into his quiet time more quickly and completely. Always be sure to provide several rounds of daily play and free time (in a fenced area or on your retractable leash) in addition to plenty of chewing materials.

Dog Talk

Dogs don't speak in words, but they do have a language—body language. They use postures, vocalizations, movements, facial gestures,

Tethering your dog is great way to keep him calm and under control, but still with you.

odors, and touch—usually with their mouths—to communicate what they are feeling and thinking.

We also "speak" using body language. We have quite an array of postures, movements, and facial gestures that accompany our touch and language as we attempt to communicate with our pets. And our dogs can quickly figure us out!

Alone, without associations, words are just noises. But, because we pair them with meaningful body language, our dogs make the connection. Dogs can really learn to understand much of what we *say*, if what we *do* at the same time is consistent.

The Positive Marker

Start your dog's education with one of the best tricks in dog training: Pair various positive reinforcers—food, a toy, touch—with a sound such as a click on a clicker (which you can get at the pet supply store) or a spoken word like "good!" or "yes!" This will enable you to later "mark" your dog's desirable behaviors.

It seems too easy: Just say "yes!" and give the dog his toy. (Or use whatever sound and reward you have chosen.) Later, when you make your marking sound right at the instant your dog does the right thing, he will know you are going to be giving him something good for that particular action. And he'll be eager to repeat the behavior to hear you mark it again!

Next, you must teach your dog to understand the meaning of cues you'll be using to ask him to perform specific behaviors. This is easy, too. Does he already do things you might like him to do on command? Of course! He lies down, he sits, he picks things up, he drops them again, he comes to you. All of the behaviors you'd like to control are already part of your dog's natural repertoire. The trick is getting him to offer those behaviors when you ask for them. And that means you have to teach him to associate a particular behavior on his part with a particular behavior on your part.

Sit Happens

Teach your dog an important new rule: From now on, he is only touched and petted when he is either sitting or lying down. You won't need to ask him to sit; in fact, you should not. Just keeping him tethered near you so there isn't much to do but stand, be ignored, or settle, and wait until sit happens.

He may pester you a bit, but be stoic and unresponsive. Starting now, when *you* are sitting down, a sitting dog is the only one you see and pay attention to. He will eventually sit, and as he does, attach the word "sit"—but don't be too excited or he'll jump right back up. Now mark with your positive sound that promises something good, then reward him with a slow, quiet, settling pet.

Training requires consistent reinforcement. Ask others to also wait until your dog is sitting and calm to touch him, and he will associate being petted with being relaxed. Be sure you train your dog to associate everyone's touch with quiet bonding.

Reinforcing "Sit" as a Command

Since your dog now understands one concept of working for a living—sit to earn petting—you can begin to shape and reinforce his desire to sit. Hold toys, treats, his bowl of food, and turn into a statue. But don't prompt him to sit! Instead, remain frozen and unavailable, looking somewhere out into space, over his head. He will put on a bit of a show, trying to get a response from you, and may offer various behaviors, but only one will push your button—sitting. Wait for him to offer the "right" behavior, and when he does, you unfreeze. Say "sit," then mark with an excited "good!" and give him the toy or treat with a release command—"OK!"

When you notice spontaneous sits occurring, be sure to take advantage of those free opportunities to make your command sequence meaningful and positive. Say "sit" as you observe sit happen—then mark with "good!" and praise, pet, or reward the dog. Soon, every time you look at your dog he'll be sitting and looking right back at you!

Now, after thirty days of purely positive practice, it's time to give him a test. When he is just walking around doing his own thing, suddenly ask him to sit. He'll probably do it right away. If he doesn't, do *not* repeat your command, or you'll just undermine its meaning ("sit" means sit *now;* the command is not "sit, sit, sit, sit"). Instead, get something he likes and let him know you have it. Wait for him to offer the sit— he will—then say "sit!" and complete your marking and rewarding sequence.

OK

"OK" will probably rate as one of your dog's favorite words. It's like the word "recess" to schoolchildren. It is the word used to release your dog from a command. You can introduce "OK" during your "sit" practice. When he gets up from a sit, say "OK" to tell him the sitting is finished. Soon that sound will mean "freedom."

Make it even more meaningful and positive. Whenever he spontaneously bounds away, say "OK!" Squeak a toy, and when he notices and shows interest, toss it for him.

Down

I've mentioned that you should only pet your dog when he is either sitting or lying down. Now, using the approach I've just introduced for "sit," teach your dog to lie down. You will be a statue, and hold something he would like to get but that you'll only release to a dog who is lying down. It helps to lower the desired item to the floor in front of him, still not speaking and not letting him have it until he offers you the new behavior you are seeking.

Lower your dog's reward to the floor to help him figure out what behavior will earn him his reward.

He may offer a sit and then wait expectantly, but you must make him keep searching for the new trick that triggers your generosity. Allow your dog to experiment and find the right answer, even if he has to search around for it first. When he lands on "down" and learns it is another behavior that works, he'll offer it more quickly the next time.

Don't say "down" until he lies down, to tightly associate your prompt with the correct behavior. To say "down, down, down" as he is sitting, looking at you, or pawing at the toy would make "down" mean those behaviors instead! Whichever behavior he offers, a training opportunity has been created. Once you've attached and shaped both sitting and lying down, you can ask for both behaviors with your verbal prompts, "sit" or "down." Be sure to only reinforce the "correct" reply!

Stay

"Stay" can easily be taught as an extension of what you've already been practicing. To teach "stay," you follow the entire sequence for reinforcing a "sit" or "down," except you wait a bit longer before you give the release word, "OK!" Wait a second or two longer during each practice before saying "OK!" and releasing your dog to the positive reinforcer (toy, treat, or one of life's other rewards).

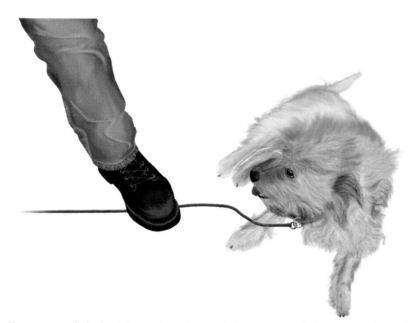

You can step on the leash to help your dog understand the down-stay, but only do this when he is already lying down. You don't want to hurt him!

If he gets up before you've said "OK," you have two choices: pretend the release was your idea and quickly interject "OK!" as he breaks; or, if he is more experienced and practiced, mark the behavior with your correction sound—"eh!"— and then gently put him back on the spot, wait for him to lie down, and begin again. Be sure the next three practices are a success. Ask him to wait for just a second, and release him before he can be wrong. You need to keep your dog feeling like more of a success than a failure as you begin to test his training in increasingly more distracting and difficult situations.

As he gets the hang of it—he stays until you say "OK"— you can gradually push for longer times—up to a minute on a sit-stay, and up to three minutes on a down-stay. You can also gradually add distractions and work in new environments. To add a minor self-correction for the down-stay, stand on the dog's leash after he lies down, allowing about three inches of slack. If tries to get up before you've said "OK," he'll discover it doesn't work.

Do not step on the leash to make your dog lie down! This could badly hurt his neck, and will destroy his trust in you. Remember, we are teaching our dogs to make the best choices, not inflicting our answers upon them!

Come

Rather than thinking of "come" as an action—"come to me"—think of it as a place—"the dog is sitting in front of me, facing me." Since your dog by now really likes sitting to earn your touch and other positive reinforcement, he's likely to sometimes sit directly in front of you, facing you, all on his own. When this happens, give it a specific name: "come."

Now follow the rest of the training steps you have learned to make him like doing it and reinforce the behavior by practicing it any chance you get. Anything your dog wants and likes could be earned as a result of his first offering the sit-in-front known as "come."

You can help guide him into the right location. Use your hands as "landing gear" and pat the insides of your legs at his nose level. Do this while backing up a bit, to help him maneuver to the straight-in-front, facing-you position. Don't say the

Pat the insides of your legs to show your dog exactly where you like him to sit when you say "come."

word "come" while he's maneuvering, because he hasn't! You are trying to make "come" the end result, not the work in progress.

You can also help your dog by marking his movement in the right direction: Use your positive sound or word to promise he is getting warm. When he finally sits facing you, enthusiastically say "come," mark again with your positive word, and release him with an enthusiastic "OK!" Make it so worth his while, with lots of play and praise, that he can't wait for you to ask him to come again!

Building a Better Recall

Practice, practice, practice. Now, practice some more. Teach your dog that all good things in life hinge upon him first sitting in front of you in a behavior named "come." When you think he really has got it, test him by asking him to "come" as you gradually add distractions and change locations. Expect setbacks as you make these changes and practice accordingly. Lower your expectations and make his task easier so he is able to get it right. Use those distractions as rewards, when they are appropriate. For example, let him check out the interesting leaf that blew by as a reward for first coming to you and ignoring it.

Add distance and call your dog to come while he is on his retractable leash. If he refuses and sits looking at you blankly, *do not* jerk, tug, "pop," or reel him in. Do nothing! It is his move; wait to see what behavior he offers. He'll either begin to approach (mark the behavior with an excited "good!"), sit and do nothing (just keep waiting), or he'll try to move in some direction other than toward you. If he tries to leave, use your correction marker—"eh!"— and bring him to a stop by letting him walk to the end of the leash, *not* by jerking him. Now walk to him in a neutral manner, and don't jerk or show any disapproval. Gently bring him back to the spot where he was when you called him, then back away and face him, still waiting and not reissuing your command. Let him keep examining his options until he finds the one that works—yours!

If you have practiced everything I've suggested so far and given your dog a chance to really learn what "come" means, he is well aware of what you want and is quite intelligently weighing all his options. The only way he'll know your way is the one that works is to be allowed to examine his other choices and discover that they *don't* work.

Sooner or later every dog tests his training. Don't be offended or angry when your dog tests you. No matter how positive you've made it, he won't always want to do everything you ask, every time. When he explores the "what happens if I don't" scenario, your training is being strengthened. He will discover through his own process of trial and error that the best—and only—way out of a command he really doesn't feel compelled to obey is to obey it.

Let's Go

Many pet owners wonder if they can retain control while walking their dogs and still allow at least some running in front, sniffing, and playing. You might worry that allowing your dog occasional freedom could result in him expecting it all the time, leading to a testy, leash-straining walk. It's possible for both parties on the leash to have an enjoyable experience by implementing and reinforcing well-thought-out training techniques.

Begin by making word associations you'll use on your walks. Give the dog some slack on the leash, and as he starts to walk away from you say "OK" and begin to follow him.

Give your dog slack on his leash as you walk and let him make the decision to walk with you.

Do not let him drag you; set the pace even when he is being given a turn at being the leader. Whenever he starts to pull, just come to a standstill and refuse to move (or refuse to allow him to continue forward) until there is slack in the leash. Do this correction without saying anything at all. When he isn't pulling, you may decide to just stand still and let him sniff about within the range the slack leash allows, or you may even mosey along following him. After a few minutes of "recess," it is time to work. Say something like "that's it" or "time's up," close the distance between you and your dog, and touch him.

Next say "let's go" (or whatever command you want to use to mean "follow me as we walk"). Turn and walk off, and, if he follows, mark his behavior with "good!" Then stop,

When your dog catches up with you, make sure you let him know what a great dog he is!

Intersperse periods of attentive walking, where your dog is on a shorter leash, with periods on a slack leash, where he is allowed to look and sniff around.

squat down, and let him catch you. Make him glad he did! Start again, and do a few transitions as he gets the hang of your follow-the-leader game, speeding up, slowing down, and trying to make it fun. When you stop, he gets to catch up and receive some deserved positive reinforcement. Don't forget that's the reason he is following you, so be sure to make it worth his while!

Require him to remain attentive to you. Do not allow sniffing, playing, eliminating, or pulling during your time as leader on a walk. If he seems to get distracted—which, by the way, is the main reason dogs walk poorly with their people—change direction or pace without saying a word. Just help him realize "oops, I lost track of my human." Do not jerk his neck and say "heel"—this will make the word "heel" mean pain in the neck and will not encourage him to cooperate with you. Don't repeat "let's go," either. He needs to figure out that it is his job to keep track of and follow you if he wants to earn the positive benefits you provide.

The best reward you can give a dog for performing an attentive, controlled walk is a few minutes of walking without all of the controls. Of course, he must remain on a leash even during the "recess" parts of the walk, but allowing him to discriminate between attentive following—"let's go"—and having a few moments of relaxation—"OK"—will increase his willingness to work.

Training for Attention

Your dog pretty much has a one-track mind. Once he is focused on something, everything else is excluded. This can be great, for instance, when he's focusing on you! But it can also be dangerous if, for example, his attention is riveted on the bunny he is chasing and he does not hear you call—that is, not unless he has been trained to pay attention when you say his name.

When you say your dog's name, you'll want him to make eye contact with you. Begin teaching this by making yourself so intriguing that he can't help but look.

When you call your dog's name, you will again be seeking a specific response—eye contact. The best way to teach this is to trigger his alerting response by making a noise with your mouth, such as whistling or a kissing sound, and then immediately doing something he'll find very intriguing.

You can play a treasure hunt game to help teach him to regard his name as a request for attention. As a bonus, you can reinforce the rest of his new vocabulary at the same time.

Treasure Hunt

Make a kissing sound, then jump up and find a dog toy or dramatically raid the fridge and rather noisily eat a piece of cheese. After doing this twice, make a kissing sound and then look at your dog.

Of course he is looking at you! He is waiting to see if that sound—the kissing sound—means you're going to go hunting again. After all, you're so good at it! Because he is looking, say his name, mark with "good," then go hunting and find his toy. Release it to him with an "OK." At any point if he follows you, attach your "let's go!" command; if he leaves you, give permission with "OK."

Using this approach, he cannot be wrong—any behavior your dog offers can be named. You can add things like "take it" when he picks up a toy, and "thank you" when he happens to drop one. Many opportunities to make your new vocabulary meaningful and positive can be found within this simple training game.

Problems to watch out for when teaching the treasure hunt:

- You really do not want your dog to come to you when you call his name (later, when you try to engage his attention to ask him to stay, he'll already be on his way toward you). You just want him to look at you.
- Saying "watch me, watch me" doesn't teach your dog to *offer* his attention. It just makes you a background noise.
- Don't lure your dog's attention with the reward. Get his attention and then reward him for looking. Try holding a toy in one hand with your arm stretched out to your side. Wait until he looks at you rather than the toy. Now say his name then mark with "good!" and release the toy. As he goes for it, say "OK."

To get your dog's attention, try holding his toy with your arm out to your side. Wait until he looks at you, then mark the moment and give him the toy.

Teaching Cooperation

Never punish your dog for failing to obey you or try to punish him into compliance. Bribing, repeating yourself, and doing a behavior for him all avoid the real issue of dog training—his will. He must be helped to be willing, not made to achieve tasks. Good dog training helps your dog want to obey. He learns that he can gain what he values most through cooperation and compliance, and can't gain those things any other way.

Your dog is learning to *earn,* rather than expect, the good things in life. And you've become much more important to him than you were before. Because you are allowing him to experiment and learn, he doesn't have to be forced, manipulated, or bribed. When he wants something, he can gain it by cooperating with you. One of those "somethings"—and a great reward you shouldn't underestimate—is your positive attention, paid to him with love and sincere approval!

Chapter 10

Housetraining Your Cavalier

Excerpted from Housetraining: An Owner's Guide to a Happy Healthy Pet, 1st Edition, *by September Morn*

By the time puppies are about 3 weeks old, they start to follow their mother around. When they are a few steps away from their clean sleeping area, the mama dog stops. The pups try to nurse but mom won't allow it. The pups mill around in frustration, then nature calls and they all urinate and defecate here, away from their bed. The mother dog returns to the nest, with her brood waddling behind her. Their first housetraining lesson has been a success.

The next one to housetrain puppies should be their breeder. The breeder watches as the puppies eliminate, then deftly removes the soiled papers and replaces them with clean papers before the pups can traipse back through their messes. He has wisely arranged the puppies' space so their bed, food, and drinking water are as far away from the elimination area as possible. This way, when the pups follow their mama, they will move away from their sleeping and eating area before eliminating. This habit will help the pups be easily housetrained.

Your Housetraining Shopping List

While your puppy's mother and breeder are getting her started on good housetraining habits, you'll need to do some shopping. If you have all the essentials in place before your dog arrives, it will be easier to help her learn the rules from day one.

Newspaper: The younger your puppy and larger her breed, the more newspapers you'll need. Newspaper is absorbent, abundant, cheap, and convenient.

Puddle Pads: If you prefer not to stockpile newspaper, a commercial alternative is puddle pads. These thick paper pads can be purchased under several trade names at pet supply stores. The pads have waterproof backing, so puppy urine doesn't seep through onto the floor. Their disadvantages are that they will cost you more than newspapers and that they contain plastics that are not biodegradable.

Poop Removal Tool: There are several types of poop removal tools available. Some are designed with a separate pan and rake, and others have the handles hinged like scissors. Some scoops need two hands for operation, while others are designed for one-handed use. Try out the different brands at your pet supply store. Put a handful of pebbles or dog kibble on the floor and then pick them up with each type of scoop to determine which works best for you.

Plastic Bags: When you take your dog outside your yard, you *must* pick up after her. Dog waste is unsightly, smelly, and can harbor disease. In many cities and towns, the law mandates dog owners clean up pet waste deposited on public ground. Picking up after your dog using a plastic bag scoop is simple. Just put your hand inside the bag, like a mitten, and then grab the droppings. Turn the bag inside out, tie the top, and that's that.

Crate: To housetrain a puppy, you will need some way to confine her when you're unable to supervise. A dog crate is a secure way to confine your dog for short periods during the day and to use as a comfortable bed at night. Crates come in wire mesh and in plastic. The wire ones are foldable to store flat in a smaller space. The plastic ones are more cozy, draft-free, and quiet, and are approved for airline travel.

Baby Gates: Since you shouldn't crate a dog for more than an hour or two at a time during the day, baby gates are a good way to limit your dog's freedom in the house. Be sure the baby gates you use are safe. The old-fashioned wooden, expanding lattice type has seriously injured a number of children by collapsing and trapping a leg, arm, or neck. That type of gate can hurt a puppy, too, so use the modern grid type gates instead. You'll need more than one baby gate if you have several doorways to close off.

Exercise Pen: Portable exercise pens are great when you have a young pup or a small dog. These metal or plastic pens are made of rectangular panels

Housetraining is simply a matter of letting your dog know what is appropriate and what is not.

that are hinged together. The pens are freestanding, sturdy, foldable, and can be carried like a suitcase. You could set one up in your kitchen as the pup's daytime corral, and then take it outdoors to contain your pup while you garden or just sit and enjoy the day.

Enzymatic Cleaner: All dogs make housetraining mistakes. Accept this and be ready for it by buying an enzymatic cleaner made especially for pet accidents. Dogs like to eliminate where they have done it before, and lingering smells lead them to those spots. Ordinary household cleaners may remove all the odors you can smell, but only an enzymatic cleaner will remove everything your dog can smell.

The First Day

Housetraining is a matter of establishing good habits in your dog. That means you never want her to learn anything she will eventually have to unlearn. Start off housetraining on the right foot by teaching your dog that you prefer her to eliminate outside. Designate a potty area in your backyard (if you have one) or in the street in front of your home and take your dog to it as soon as you arrive home. Let her sniff a bit and, when she squats to go, give the action a name:

Don't Overuse the Crate

A crate serves well as a dog's overnight bed, but you should not leave the dog in her crate for more than an hour or two during the day. Throughout the day, she needs to play and exercise. She is likely to want to drink some water and will undoubtedly eliminate. Confining your dog all day will give her no option but to soil her crate. This is not just unpleasant for you and the dog, but it reinforces bad cleanliness habits. And crating a pup for the whole day is abusive. Don't do it.

"potty" or "do it" or anything else you won't be embarrassed to say in public. Eventually your dog will associate that word with the act and will eliminate on command. When she's finished, praise her with "good potty!"

That first day, take your puppy out to the potty area frequently. Although she may not eliminate every time, you are establishing a routine: You take her to her spot, ask her to eliminate, and praise her when she does.

Just before bedtime, take your dog to her potty area once more. Stand by and wait until she produces. Do not put your dog to bed for the night until she has eliminated. Be patient and calm. This is not the time to play with or excite your dog. If she's too excited, a pup not only won't eliminate, she probably won't want to sleep either.

Most dogs, even young ones, will not soil their beds if they can avoid it. For this reason, a sleeping crate can be a tremendous help during housetraining. Being crated at night can help a dog develop the muscles that control elimination. So after your dog has emptied out, put her to bed in her crate.

A good place to put your dog's sleeping crate is near your own bed. Dogs are pack animals, so they feel safer sleeping with others in a common area. In your bedroom, the pup will be near you and you'll be close enough to hear when she wakes during the night and needs to eliminate.

Pups under 4 months old often are not able to hold their urine all night. If your puppy has settled down to sleep but awakens and fusses a few hours later, she probably needs to go out. For the best housetraining progress, take your pup to her elimination area whenever she needs to go, even in the wee hours of the morning.

Your pup may soil in her crate if you ignore her late night urgency. It's unfair to let this happen, and it sends the wrong message about your expectations for

Take your dog to her potty spot first thing every morning.

cleanliness. Resign yourself to this midnight outing and just get up and take the pup out. Your pup will outgrow this need soon and will learn in the process that she can count on you, and you'll wake happily each morning to a clean dog.

The next morning, the very first order of business is to take your pup out to eliminate. Don't forget to take her to her special potty spot, ask her to eliminate, and then praise her when she does. After your pup empties out in the morning, give her breakfast, and then take her to her potty area again. After that, she shouldn't need to eliminate again right away, so you can allow her some free playtime. Keep an eye on the pup though, because when she pauses in play she may need to go potty. Take her to the right spot, give the command, and praise if she produces.

Confine Your Pup

A pup or dog who has not finished housetraining should *never* be allowed the run of the house unattended. A new dog (especially a puppy) with unlimited access to your house will make her own choices about where to eliminate. Vigilance during your dog's first few weeks in your home will pay big dividends. Every potty mistake delays housetraining; every success speeds it along.

Prevent problems by setting up a controlled environment for your new pet. A good place for a puppy corral is often the kitchen. Kitchens almost always have waterproof or easily cleaned floors, which is a distinct asset with leaky pups. A bathroom, laundry room, or enclosed porch could be used for a puppy corral, but the kitchen is generally the best location. Kitchens are a meeting place and a hub of activity for many families, and a puppy will learn better manners when she is socialized thoroughly with family, friends, and nice strangers.

The way you structure your pup's corral area is very important. Her bed, food, and water should be at the opposite end of the corral from the potty area. When you first get your pup, spread newspaper over the rest of the floor of her playpen corral. Lay the papers at least four pages thick and be sure to overlap the edges. As you note the pup's progress, you can remove the papers nearest the sleeping and eating corner. Gradually decrease the size of the papered area until only the end where you want the pup to eliminate is covered. If you will be training your dog to eliminate outside, place newspaper at the end of the corral that is closest to the door that leads outdoors. That way as she moves away from the clean area to the papered area, the pup will also form the habit of heading toward the door to go out.

Maintain a scent marker for the pup's potty area by reserving a small soiled piece of paper when you clean up. Place this piece, with her scent of urine, under the top sheet of the clean papers you spread. This will cue your pup where to eliminate.

Most dog owners use a combination of indoor papers and outdoor elimination areas. When the pup is left by herself in the corral, she can potty on the ever-present newspaper. When you are available to take the pup outside, she can do her business in the outdoor spot. It is not difficult to switch a pup from indoor paper training to outdoor elimination. Use the papers as long as your pup needs them. If you come home and they haven't been soiled, you are ahead.

> ### TIP
>
> **Water**
>
> Make sure your dog has access to clean water at all times. Limiting the amount of water a dog drinks is not necessary for housetraining success and can be very dangerous. A dog needs water to digest food, to maintain a proper body temperature and proper blood volume, and to clean her system of toxins and wastes. A healthy dog will automatically drink the right amount. Do not restrict water intake. Controlling your dog's access to water is not the key to housetraining her; controlling her access to everything else in your home is.

When setting up your pup's outdoor yard, put the lounging area as far away as possible from the potty area, just as with the indoor corral setup. People with large yards, for example, might leave a patch unmowed at the edge of the lawn to serve as the dog's elimination area. Other dog owners teach the dog to relieve herself in a designated corner of a deck or patio. For an apartment-dwelling city dog, the outdoor potty area might be a tiny balcony or the curb. Each dog owner has somewhat different expectations for their dog. Teach your dog to eliminate in a spot that suits your environment and lifestyle.

Be sure to pick up droppings in your yard at least once a day. Dogs have a natural desire to stay far away from their own excrement, and if too many piles litter the ground, your dog won't want to walk through it and will start eliminating elsewhere. Leave just one small piece of feces in the potty area to remind your dog where the right spot is located.

To help a pup adapt to the change from indoors to outdoors, take one of her potty papers outside to the new elimination area. Let the pup stand on the paper when she goes potty outdoors. Each day for four days, reduce the size of the paper by half. By the fifth day, the pup, having used a smaller and smaller piece of paper to stand on, will probably just go to that spot and eliminate.

Take your pup to her outdoor potty place frequently throughout the day. A puppy can hold her urine for only about as many hours as her age in months, and will move her bowels as many times a day as she eats. So a 2-month-old pup will urinate about every two hours, while at 4 months she can manage about four hours between piddles. Pups vary somewhat in their rate of development, so this is not a hard and fast rule. It does, however, present a realistic idea of how long a pup can be left without access to a potty place. Past 4 months, her potty trips will be less frequent.

Pick a potty spot in the yard or on the deck and take your dog to that spot consistently.

When you take the dog outdoors to her spot, keep her leashed so that she won't wander away. Stand quietly and let her sniff around in the designated area. If your pup starts to leave before she has eliminated, gently lead her back and remind her to go. If your pup sniffs at the spot, praise her calmly, say the command word, and just wait. If she produces, praise serenely, then give her time to sniff around a little more. She may not be finished, so give her time to go again before allowing her to play and explore her new home.

If you find yourself waiting more than five minutes for your dog to potty, take her back inside. Watch your pup carefully for twenty minutes, not giving her any opportunity to slip away to eliminate unnoticed. If you are too busy to watch the pup, put her in her crate. After twenty minutes, take her to the outdoor potty spot again and tell her what to do. If you're unsuccessful after five minutes, crate the dog again. Give her another chance to eliminate in fifteen or twenty minutes. Eventually, she will have to go.

Watch Your Pup

Keep a chart of your new dog's elimination behavior for the first three or four days. Jot down what times she eats, sleeps, and eliminates. After several days a pattern will emerge that can help you determine your pup's body rhythms. Most dogs tend to eliminate at fairly regular intervals. Once you know your new dog's natural rhythms, you'll be able to anticipate her needs and schedule appropriate potty outings.

Understanding the meanings of your dog's postures can also help you win the battle of the puddle. When your dog is getting ready to eliminate, she will display a specific set of postures. The sooner you can learn to read these signals, the cleaner your floor will stay.

A young puppy who feels the urge to eliminate may start to sniff the ground and walk in a circle. If the pup is very young, she may simply squat and go. All young puppies, male or female, squat to urinate. If you are housetraining a pup under 4 months of age, regardless of sex, watch for the beginnings of a squat as the signal to rush the pup to the potty area.

When a puppy is getting ready to defecate, she may run urgently back and forth or turn in a circle while sniffing or starting to squat. If defecation is imminent, the pup's anus may protrude or open slightly. When she starts to go, the pup will squat and hunch her back, her tail sticking straight out behind. There is no mistaking this posture; nothing else looks like this. If your pup takes this position, take her to her potty area. Hurry! You may have to carry her.

A young puppy won't have much time between feeling the urge and actually eliminating, so you'll have to be quick to note her postural clues and intercept your pup in time. Pups from 3 to 6 months have a few seconds more between the urge and the act than younger ones do. The older your pup, the more time you'll have to get her to the potty area after she begins the posture signals that alert you to her need.

Accidents Happen

If you see your pup about to eliminate somewhere other than the designated area, interrupt her immediately. Say "wait, wait, wait!" or clap your hands loudly to startle her into stopping. Carry the pup, if she's still small enough, or take her collar and lead her to the correct area. Once your dog is in the potty area, give her the command to eliminate. Use a friendly voice for the command, then wait patiently for her to produce. The pup may be tense because you've just startled her and may have to relax a bit before she's able to eliminate. When she does her job, include the command word in the praise you give ("good potty").

Make sure your pup knows why she's outside; praise her when she eliminates in the right place.

The old-fashioned way of housetraining involved punishing a dog's mistakes even before she knew what she was supposed to do. Puppies were punished for breaking rules they didn't understand about functions they couldn't control. This was not fair. While your dog is new to housetraining, there is no need or excuse for punishing her mistakes. Your job is to take the dog to the potty area just before she needs to go, especially with pups under 3 months old. If you aren't watching your pup closely enough and she has an accident, don't punish her for your failure to anticipate her needs. It's not the pup's fault; it's yours.

In any case, punishment is not an effective tool for housetraining most dogs. Many will react to punishment by hiding puddles and feces where you won't find them right away (like behind the couch or under the desk). This eventually may lead to punishment after the fact, which leads to more hiding, and so on.

Stay a step ahead of accidents by learning to anticipate your pup's needs. Accompany your dog to the designated potty area when she needs to go. Tell her what you want her to do and praise her when she goes. This will work wonders. Punishment won't be necessary if you are a good teacher.

What happens if you come upon a mess after the fact? Some trainers say a dog can't remember having eliminated, even a few moments after she has done so. This is not true. The fact is that urine and feces carry a dog's unique scent, which she (and every other dog) can instantly recognize. So, if you happen upon a potty mistake after the fact you can still use it to teach your dog.

But remember, no punishment! Spanking, hitting, shaking, or scaring a puppy for having a housetraining accident is confusing and counterproductive. Spend your energy instead on positive forms of teaching.

Take your pup and a paper towel to the mess. Point to the urine or feces and calmly tell your puppy, "no potty here." Then scoop or sop up the accident with the paper towel. Take the evidence and the pup to the approved potty area. Drop the mess on the ground and tell the dog, "good potty here," as if she had done the deed in the right place. If your pup sniffs at the evidence, praise her calmly. If the accident happened very recently your dog may not have to go yet, but wait with her a few minutes anyway. If she eliminates, praise her. Afterwards, go finish cleaning up the mess.

Soon the puppy will understand that there is a place where you are pleased about elimination and other places where you are not. Praising for elimination in the approved place will help your pup remember the rules.

Scheduling Basics

With a new puppy in the home, don't be surprised if your rising time is suddenly a little earlier than you've been accustomed to. Puppies have earned a reputation as very early risers. When your pup wakes you at the crack of dawn, you will have to get up and take her to her elimination spot. Be patient. When your dog is an adult, she may enjoy sleeping in as much as you do.

Dogs generally have to eliminate after they play, after they nap, and after they eat.

At the end of the chapter, you'll find a typical housetraining schedule for puppies aged 10 weeks to 6 months. (To find schedules for younger and older pups, and for adult dogs, visit this book's companion web site.) It's fine to adjust the rising times when using this schedule, but you should not adjust the intervals between feedings and potty outings unless your pup's behavior justifies a change. Your puppy can only meet your expectations in housetraining if you help her learn the rules.

The schedule for puppies is devised with the assumption that someone will be home most of the time with the pup. That would be the best scenario, of course, but is not always possible. You may be able to ease the problems of a latchkey pup by having a neighbor or friend look in on the pup at noon and take her to eliminate. A better solution might be hiring a pet sitter to drop by midday. A professional pet sitter will be knowledgeable about companion animals and can give your pup high-quality care and socialization. Some can even help train your pup in both potty manners and basic obedience. Ask your veterinarian and your dog-owning friends to recommend a good pet sitter.

If you must leave your pup alone during her early housetraining period, be sure to cover the entire floor of her corral with thick layers of overlapping newspaper. If you come home to messes in the puppy corral, just clean them up. Be patient—she's still a baby.

Use this schedule (and the ones on the companion web site) as a basic plan to help prevent housetraining accidents. Meanwhile, use your own powers of observation to discover how to best modify the basic schedule to fit your dog's unique needs. Each dog is an individual and will have her own rhythms, and each dog is reliable at a different age.

Schedule for Pups 10 Weeks to 6 Months

7:00 a.m.	Get up and take the puppy from her sleeping crate to her potty spot.
7:15	Clean up last night's messes, if any.
7:30	Food and fresh water.
7:45	Pick up the food bowl. Take the pup to her potty spot; wait and praise.
8:00	The pup plays around your feet while you have your breakfast.

9:00	Potty break (younger pups may not be able to wait this long).
9:15	Play and obedience practice.
10:00	Potty break.
10:15	The puppy is in her corral with safe toys to chew and play with.
11:30	Potty break (younger pups may not be able to wait this long).
11:45	Food and fresh water.
12:00 p.m.	Pick up the food bowl and take the pup to her potty spot.
12:15	The puppy is in her corral with safe toys to chew and play with.
1:00	Potty break (younger pups may not be able to wait this long).
1:15	Put the pup on a leash and take her around the house with you.
3:30	Potty break (younger pups may not be able to wait this long).
3:45	Put the pup in her corral with safe toys and chews for solitary play and/or a nap.
4:45	Potty break.
5:00	Food and fresh water.
5:15	Potty break.
5:30	The pup may play nearby (either leashed or in her corral) while you prepare your evening meal.
7:00	Potty break.
7:15	Leashed or closely watched, the pup may play and socialize with family and visitors.
9:15	Potty break (younger pups may not be able to wait this long).
10:45	Last chance to potty.
11:00	Put the pup to bed in her crate for the night.

Appendix

Learning More About Your Cavalier King Charles Spaniel

Some Good Books

For an in-depth look at Cavaliers, there are three books I recommend highly. They are written by breeders from Britain, where the Cavalier originated, and the authors are international breed judges.

Evans, John, *Cavalier King Charles Spaniels: An Owner's Companion,* Trafalgar Square Publishing, 1995.

Field, Bruce, *The Cavalier King Charles Spaniel,* revised edition, Robert Hale Ltd., 2001.

Smith, Sheila, *Cavalier King Charles Spaniels Today,* Ringpress Books, 2002.

About Health Care

Arden, Darlene, *The Angell Memorial Animal Hospital Book of Wellness and Preventive Care for Dogs,* Contemporary Books, 2003.

Bamberger, Michelle, DVM, *Help! The Quick Guide to First Aid for Your Dog,* Howell Book House, 1995.

Messonnier, Shawn, DVM, *8 Weeks to a Healthy Dog,* Rodale, 2003.

Shojai, Amy, *Complete Care for Your Aging Dog,* New American Library, 2003.

About Training

McCullough, Susan, *Housetraining For Dummies,* Wiley Publishing, 2002.

Ross, John and Barbara McKinney, *Dog Talk: Training Your Dog Through a Canine Point of View,* St. Martin's Press, 1995.

Rutherford, Clarice, and David H. Neil, MRCVS, *How to Raise a Puppy You Can Live With*, Alpine Publications, 1999.

Smith, Cheryl S., *The Rosetta Bone—The Key to Communication Between Humans and Canines*, Howell Book House, 2004.

Canine Activities

Burch, Mary, *Wanted: Animal Volunteers*, Howell Book House, 2002.

Hall, Lynn, *Dog Showing for Beginners*, Howell Book House, 1994.

O'Neil, Jacqueline F. *All About Agility*, Howell Book House, 1999.

Volhard, Jack and Wendy, *The Canine Good Citizen: Every Dog Can Be One*, 2nd ed., Howell Book House, 1997.

Magazines

AKC Gazette
AKC Family Dog
American Kennel Club
260 Madison Avenue
New York, NY 10016
(212) 696-8200
www.akc.org

Dog Fancy
P.O. Box 37185
Boone, IA 50037-0185.
(800) 896-4939
www.dogfancy.com

Dog Watch
P.O. Box 420235
Palm Coast, FL 32142-0235
(800) 829-5574
www.vet.cornell.edu/public
resources/dog.htm#ifo

DogWorld
P.O. Box 37186
Boone, IA 50037-0186
(800) 896-4939
www.dogworldmag.com

The Royal Spaniels
14531 Jefferson Street
Midway City, CA 92655
(714) 893-0053
www.the-royal-spaniels.com

Registries

There are two major organizations that register Cavaliers in the United States. The original club, the Cavalier King Charles Spaniel Club USA Inc., was established in

1956 and is not affiliated with the AKC. It has had the welfare of the breed at heart since it was founded in the early 1950s. The American Cavalier King Charles Spaniel Club, established in 1994 by a group of well-respected breeders, is affiliated with the AKC. The Cavalier King Charles Spaniel Club of Canada, established in 1973, is affiliated with the Canadian Kennel Club.

The web sites of all three clubs are worth investigating, because they include resources for breeder referrals and rescue groups, list affiliated regional clubs and contact persons, and many interesting articles about the breed.

American Kennel Club (AKC)
260 Madison Avenue
New York, NY 10016
(212) 696-8200
www.akc.org

Cavalier King Charles Spaniel Club USA Inc.
www.ckcsc.org

American Cavalier King Charles Spaniel Club
www.ackcsc.org

Cavalier King Charles Spaniel Club of Canada
www.candog.com/cavaliers

Internet Resources

American Society for the Prevention of Cruelty to Animals
www.aspca.org
Features humane education and advocacy information, with a link to the ASPCA Poison Control Center.

American Veterinary Medical Association
www.avma.org
The latest veterinary medical news.

Canine Freestyle Federation
www.canine-freestyle.com
This site is devoted to canine freestyle—dancing with your dog. There's information about freestyle events, tips, and even music to choose!

The Cavalier Connection
www.ckcs.com
An online community for the care and ownership of the Cavalier King Charles Spaniel.

Dog Friendly
www.dogfriendly.com
Information about traveling with dogs, including guidebooks.

Index

Photo Credits:

Kent Dannen: 16, 28, 44–45, 58, 60, 88, 101; *Jean M. Fogle:* 15, 36, 46, 49, 65, 92, 104–105; *Neil Kinnear and Lesley Chung:* 23; *Norma Moffat:* 17, 19, 20, 24, 25, 26, 31, 33, 34, 37, 38, 53, 56, 61, 62, 68, 69, 84, 93, 94, 102, 106, 126, 130, 132, 134, 135; *Bonnie Nance:* title page, 4–5, 8–9, 11, 12, 28, 39, 43, 51, 52, 66, 72, 73, 74, 75, 76, 78, 85, 90, 95, 100, 128